WELSH IN THE TWENTY-FIRST CENTURY

WELSH IN THE TWENTY-FIRST CENTURY

Edited by

Delyth Morris

CARDIFF
UNIVERSITY OF WALES PRESS
2010

Er cof am fy nhad a mam, Arthur a Catherine Lloyd, Bryngwran

© Delyth Morris, 2010

All rights reserved. No part of this book may be reproduced in any material form (including photocopying or storing it in any medium by electronic means and whether or not transiently or incidentally to some other use of this publication) without the written permission of the copyright owner except in accordance with the provisions of the Copyright, Designs and Patents Act 1988. Applications for the copyright owner's written permission to reproduce any part of this publication should be addressed to The University of Wales Press, 10 Columbus Walk, Brigantine Place, Cardiff, CF10 4UP.

www.uwp.co.uk

British Library Cataloguing-in-Publication Data
A catalogue record for this book is available from the British Library.

ISBN 978-0-7083-2299-4
e-ISBN 978-0-7083-2300-7

The right of Delyth Morris to be identified as copyright holder of this work has been asserted by her in accordance with sections 77, 78 and 79 of the Copyright, Designs and Patents Act 1988.

Printed by CPI Antony Rowe, Chippenham, Wiltshire

Contents

Foreword *Padraig Ó Riagáin*	ix
Introduction *Delyth Morris*	1
Language, Meaning and the Knowledge Economy *Glyn Williams*	7
From Act to Action in Wales *Colin H. Williams*	36
Increasing Bilingualism in Bilingual Education *Colin Baker*	61
Young People and their Use of the Welsh Language *Delyth Morris*	80
Children's Acquisition of Welsh in a Bilingual Setting: A Psycholinguistic Perspective *Enlli Môn Thomas and Robert Mayr*	99
Welsh Speakers: Age Profile and Out-Migration *Hywel M. Jones*	118
Attitudes to Language and Bilingualism among English In-Migrants to North Wales *Howard Davis, Graham Day and Angela Drakakis-Smith*	148
Index	169

Foreword

As an Irish academic whose primary interest concerns minority language policy, I have long been an intent observer of related research on the other side of the Irish sea. There are, of course, differences between the Irish and Welsh cases in terms of both the linguistic and policy context. But these differences are more than balanced by many historical and structural similarities. Thus I have been much more than a detached observer. I have learned a great deal from the theoretical schemes, methodological approaches and empirical findings of my Welsh counterparts. In time, this interest was strengthened and consolidated by friendships and collaborative research projects. For many reasons, therefore, it gives me great pleasure to contribute a foreword to this collection of papers. The professional rewards of reading a set of well-constructed papers are always, as in this case, enhanced by personal acquaintance with most of the authors and a sense that we share many of the same concerns regarding the language communities within which we all live and work.

In a piece that he wrote for the *Annual Review of Sociology* in 1985, Joshua Fishman saw virtue in the interdisciplinary nature of the field known as sociolinguistics or sociology of language. But he also lamented what he saw as the reluctance of one discipline, sociology, to accept co-responsibility for the development of the of the 'sociolinguistic enterprise'. Whatever justification there was to judge the relative contribution of the various disciplines in the United States between the 1960s and the 1980s in this fashion, I don't think that that the same could have been said about the state of the discipline in Wales or, indeed, Ireland in the same period or since. In 1975, a decade before Fishman wrote his review, Hechter had already published his study of *Internal Colonialism: The Celtic Fringe in British Development*, a book in which he not only looked at the relationship between the economy, economic development, population movements and language, but also introduced the very useful concept of the cultural division of labour into sociology of language. In 1987 and 1988 two issues of *The International Journal of the Sociology of Language,* a journal of which Fishman was, and is, general editor, were devoted to Wales and Ireland respectively, and they included many contributions by sociologists and other members of the social science family of disciplines. I am not, of course, arguing that those trained in linguistics were not also contributing to the 'sociolinguistic enterprise' in Wales, but simply that the social science perspective has been a prominent feature in the development of this field in Wales for many decades and, if we accept Fishman's assessment, this alone makes the nature and character of socioloinguistic research in Wales different from the United States.

The other distinguishing feature of the Welsh research represented in this volume is its engagement with, and concern for, contemporary policy issues. While the titles may suggest a predominantly academic interest, a closer reading will nearly always show a pronounced sensitivity for the well-being of the language community under study and the urgent need to design appropriate policy interventions. A few examples may suffice. The paper by Hywel Jones is a detailed piece of demographic research which examines the relationship between out-migration and the age of Welsh speakers. While any researcher could fully justify the selection of this research topic on academic grounds alone, the author in this case remarks towards the end that 'one stimulus for this analysis is the importance of the traditionally Welsh-speaking area for the future of the Welsh language'. A second example can be seen in Delyth Morris's paper on young people's social networks and their use of language within those networks. Again the academic credentials of this piece are impeccable. Nonetheless, the reason the research was undertaken was because of concern that 'young people's knowledge of Welsh does not translate into use'. This is, of course, also a critical policy issue in many minority language contexts. The remaining papers focus on topics of equal relevance to the concerns of policy-makers and the Welsh-language community in general. They include bilingual education, attittudes of in-migrants to language issues, acquiring Welsh in a bilingual setting, language and the knowledge economy and language-planning institutions and legislation. Even a more obviously theoretical piece, like Glyn Williams's reflections on language, meaning and the knowledge economy, also includes a discussion of the implication of his theorizing for education, language planning and the economy in Wales.

At the same time, it is necessary to stress that the sociology of language in Wales is no local matter. All of the research here draws on the resources of theoretical and methodological work worldwide and, confidently and deliberately seeks to enhance that corpus, while at the same time addressing local concerns. Thus the present volume continues the tradition of earlier work at many levels . It is interdisciplinary, but predominantly within the social science stable. All of the authors have already contributed a great deal to the development of the field, and the present volume shows both some of their present preoccupations as well as, in part, revisiting previous work. For the reader who is looking for an introduction to a well-developed body of research in the field of sociology of language and, at the same time, to a regional language community with no mean record in the field of policy innovation and implementation, the book is ideal. I wholeheartedly welcome it, and I compliment Delyth and her co-authors on their achievement.

Padraig Ó Riagáin
Trinity College Dublin

Introduction

Delyth Morris
School of Social Sciences
Bangor University

The idea for a collection of papers looking at the Welsh language at the beginning of the twenty-first century was first suggested by the economist Roy Thomas at a meeting of the Economics and Sociology Section of the University of Wales Guild of Graduates in November 2006. The imminent demise of the University of Wales as a federal institution meant that it was only a matter of time until the Economics and Sociology Section also ceased to exist, and it was felt that there was a need to mark the occasion. The section was established at the beginning of the 1950s, with the aim of discussing the economy and society of Wales, mainly through the medium of Welsh, and over the years it has published various papers on a number of relevant topics. It was felt therefore that a collection of papers which looked at the sociology of Welsh at the beginning of the twenty-first century would be a fitting tribute to the work of academics who had contributed to this respected forum for over fifty years. It was also noted that more than two decades had gone by since Glyn Williams edited the important edition of the *International Journal of the Sociology of Language*, on *The Sociology of Welsh* in 1987, and therefore it was felt that another collection of papers in this area was timely.

Glyn Williams is undoubtedly Wales's foremost sociologist of language, and the most astute analyst of the Welsh language in its European context. It is fitting therefore that the volume begins with his insightful paper on language, meaning and the knowledge economy. In this paper, he looks at the value of language in the new economy, while also showing how the traditional approach to the relationship between language, economy and society has changed over the years. Williams demonstrates how we have been obliged to reformulate our understanding of language and its relevance in our lives, and the way language can play a new and profitable role in this new context. He offers a perceptive analysis of the implications for the Welsh language in three important areas – education, language planning and the economy – arguing that we need to emphasize 'shared meaning' in the teaching of languages rather than being preoccupied with issues of 'language purity'. This is an issue that places him at odds with a powerful lobby of Welsh academics and pundits, but I suspect that he would not find this position too uncomfortable! He also advocates a departure from the rigidity of the concepts of 'language maintenance and language shift', which again will be unnerving for many language planners in Wales. In considering the central role of the economy and the changing role of the state within the global economy, Williams maintains that Welsh should be viewed not as a minority language, but rather as one of several languages facing a new world economic order. Finally he highlights the huge potential for the Welsh language of the cultural economy and the creative economy in the new global order and the development of new technology. As always, Williams is stimulating and challenging in his approach, and his paper sets the rapidly changing context for the Welsh language at the beginning of the twenty-first century.

In the next paper, Colin Williams considers the implementation of the 1993 Welsh Language Act and its effects on the public sector in Wales. Drawing on research work carried out over three years with policy-makers, language officers, and staff of the Welsh Language Board, he considers the nature of the present provision and of the attitudes of staff who are invested with the duty of implementing Welsh-language plans. The views of individual customers were not canvassed. Concentrating upon a number of case studies of public authorities and agencies, he finds that the implementation of their Welsh-language plans are patchy and inconsistent, with some authorities in the north-west going beyond what is expected of them, while authorities in other areas lag a considerable way behind. Generally, there is a severe lack of appropriately skilled staff, training, and resources, which are compounded in some cases by a lack of will and political leadership. Williams discovers that the successful implementation of the 1993 legislation still depends much on good will and voluntary co-operation. He notes that the main weakness of the present legislation is that it does not afford rights to the individual, and suggests that the establishment of a language commissioner would be an important step in the right direction. In a changing linguistic landscape, the functioning of the Commission for Equality and Human Rights, the Single Equality Measure, new discrimination legislation to incorporate language, the need for further enforcement powers to ensure compliance, and so on, will all play a part in moving the agenda forward. Williams notes that there is still a lot to do in changing the attitudes and expectations of a number of players in the system, and concludes that while legislation is important, ultimately it is the socialization process in a strong civil society, particularly in education, that will ensure that people learn Welsh and learn to use it.

The education system has long been viewed as a central institution in the reproduction of the Welsh language, and the issue of Welsh and bilingualism within the education system is the theme of the next paper by Colin Baker. Although Wales has a system of bilingual education that is internationally renowned, yet, as Baker notes, surprisingly little detailed research has been carried out into teacher experiences in the field of bilingual education over the past seventy years. He maintains that we do not therefore know what works best, for whom, and why – in fact, as he notes, we do not now know much more than the 'Ministry of Education inspectors who visited Ysgol Gymraeg Aberystwyth back in February 1948'. Baker describes the ambiguity surrounding the use of 'bilingual' and 'Welsh-medium' to describe schools in Wales, and notes that even in the so-called 'Welsh-medium' schools, it has long been the practice to teach in English also. He outlines the different practices encountered in different schools in Wales, and notes that since a 'bilingual school is not an island', external issues of language status, language policy and language planning are bound to impinge on the situation faced daily by teachers in schools in Wales. Comparing with the situation in the US, he discusses the different forms of bilingual teaching and the different teaching methods employed under the 'bilingual education' banner in Wales. He stresses that we need to be clear whether we aim to teach Welsh, or a bilingual competence, in Wales's schools. If we opt for the latter, Baker appends a 'health warning' regarding the inclination of young bilingual Welsh/English-speakers to switch increasingly to using English with their peers as they grow up. If schools do not succeed in establishing Welsh as the language of communication between pupils within schools – and it is questionable whether this is possible in a 'bilingual' classroom situation – then the long-term implications for the Welsh language are bleak.

In the next paper, Morris looks at this particular group of young bilingual Welsh/English-speakers and the use they make of the Welsh language in their day-to-day lives. She discusses the results of a study carried out between 2003 and 2005 on the social networks of young people aged between thirteen and seventeen years in twelve different areas of Wales, and looks at their use of Welsh in different social contexts – the home and family, friends and contemporaries, the community, and social clubs and organizations. The participants in the study were selected on the basis of their own Welsh-language competence and that of their parents, and the results of the study show quite different responses in the different localities. While the home was the major determinant of the Welsh-language density of the young people's social networks, the linguistic nature of the respondents' home area was also a significant factor in the opportunities they had to use Welsh socially. The research allowed the development of a typology of locations, distinguished by the use of Welsh in different social networks. Three types of communities emerged: firstly, those which integrated English-language-speakers; secondly, those communities that contained two distinct and separate Welsh- and English-language groups; and thirdly, communities where Welsh was rapidly being assimilated into the normative context, with English as the predominant language. Morris concludes that there is ample evidence of the need to increase the number of situations where the use of Welsh is normative. As well as increasing opportunities for young people to use Welsh in leisure activities, she asserts that it is also extremely important to maintain the significant social institutions that reinforce Welsh in community life, particularly in schools and their associated extracurricular Welsh-medium activities.

Thomas and Mayr's paper turns the focus on to the process of young children's acquisition of mutation and grammatical gender in Welsh. Using evidence from recent studies, they consider three main issues: the nature of children's linguistic knowledge, their rate of learning, and the role that the amount of input received, particularly from the school, plays in this learning. The authors show that children often do not learn the 'rules' of mutation and gender until they are between nine to eleven years of age, and that their competence depends very much on the input of Welsh they obtain from their immediate environment. The authors conclude that families need the additional support of schools and extracurricular activities in order to ensure that children in Wales acquire a native-like proficiency in Welsh, reiterating the conclusions of Morris in the previous paper.

In his paper on Welsh-speakers and out-migration, Jones shows that the lower than expected numbers of young adult Welsh-speakers in the 2001 Census are a consequence of out-migration, rather than a failure by individuals to retain their Welsh-speaking ability. Using statistics from the 2001 Census, he considers the twin issues of in-migration and out-migration, and demonstrates how young adult Welsh speakers who were born outside Wales are more likely to move out of Wales in their early adulthood than those who are Welsh-born. One reason may be the lack of career opportunities for highly skilled people in the Welsh-speaking areas, and another is weak social ties. His observations in this respect are supported by evidence provided in the next paper by Davis, Day and Drakakis-Smith on the attitudes of English in-migrants to north Wales to issues of Welsh and bilingualism. Jones notes the importance of the traditionally Welsh-speaking areas for the future of the Welsh language, and states that the low rates of linguistic integration of people born outside Wales are the major reason why the percentage able to speak Welsh in the traditionally Welsh-speaking area has been falling.

The study by Davis, Day and Drakakis-Smith of 260 English in-migrants to the Welsh-speaking areas of north-west Wales asserts that that their attitude to the Welsh language is generally positive. That is not to say of course that positive attitudes lead to positive actions, as other research has suggested, and indeed, the authors themselves point out that despite a positive attitude, few of the in-migrants have actually succeeded in learning Welsh. In the previous paper, Jones shows how just 5 per cent of the population of Wales aged 45–64 can speak Welsh. Davis, Day and Drakakis-Smith acknowledge that the in-migrants' ease of access to English language networks and culture acts as a disincentive for linguistic integration. Although the importance of a bilingual education system is generally accepted by the respondents, it is significant that a substantial proportion of those respondents with children had them educated elsewhere in the area, in non-Welsh-medium independent or boarding schools. As the authors point out, education provides the key institution for the integration of the younger generation and their acquisition of the Welsh language, but obviously for those educated outside the local state system their opportunities for integration are significantly lower.

This collection of papers shows how events have moved on from the situation described by Glyn Williams in 1987. At that time, no comprehensive Welsh-language-use survey had been carried out; there was reluctance on the part of the state to give a lead on Welsh-medium education; and the status of the language varied greatly between locations within Wales. By now, several Welsh-language-use surveys have been carried out; the Welsh language is enjoying a heightened prestige, partly as a result of the Welsh Language Act 1993, the establishment of the Welsh Language Board in 1993 and the Welsh Assembly in 1999; and there is more uniform Welsh-language provision in public services and education throughout Wales. The announcement of the Welsh Language Measure in March 2010 is also significant. However, some things remain the same. There are still major concerns over the weakening abilities of the family and the community to reproduce the Welsh language; there is continued in-migration of non-Welsh speakers and out-migration of Welsh speakers; and there is still reluctance by many with a Welsh-language ability to use the language in their day-to-day lives. It is possible that the new emerging knowledge economy will provide better opportunities for people to use Welsh profitably, and that this in turn will have an effect on language-use patterns; it is also possible that new Welsh-language legislation will establish individual language rights, giving Welsh speakers the confidence to use the language in their dealings with the private sector as well as the public sector. The rapidly changing social and political landscape in Wales makes this an exciting time. It is hoped that this collection of papers, by providing an insight into the position of the Welsh language at the beginning of the twenty-first century, feeds into the ongoing language debate in that context in a constructive and stimulating way.

Language, Meaning and the Knowledge Economy

Glyn Williams
Centre for European Research

Introduction

We are at the cusp of change, from one variety of capitalism to another. It involves new roles for the state, new relations of production and new forces of production. It reverberates in how the various social science disciplines change, and how new forms of the understanding of language appear.

The reference point for the change is that which is referred to as immaterial labour, which is defined as the activity of the manipulation of symbols. Immaterial labour involves two different components. The informational content of the commodity refers directly to how skills increasingly involve computer use and both horizontal and vertical communication, while the activity that generates the cultural content of the commodity involves activities not usually recognized as 'work' – the definition and fixing of cultural standards, fashions, tastes, consumer norms and public opinion.

A major architect of the more recent developments was Robert Reich, secretary of labour in the USA under President Clinton. Reich argued that in the long run immaterial labour would be crucial for all economies. It involves scientific and technological research, training of the labour force, development of management, communication and electronic financial networks. Those jobs operating intellectual labour included researchers, engineers, computer scientists, lawyers, creative accountants, financial advisers, publicists, editors and journalists and university academic staff. The growth of such activities would run parallel to a decline in Tayloristic activities since such repetitive and executive activities could be easily reproduced in states with low labour costs. He further argued that globalization had removed the link between the state and the ownership of capital and the means of production. Rather, what is important is efficiency and the productivity of communication, with capital being owned by multinational corporations. What is lost through the denationalization of the ownership of capital is compensated for by the ownership of immaterial labour, of the control of knowledge production. Knowledge becomes nationalized and its organization is managed nationally. Thus the state should invest strategically in value-creating activities, the immaterial activities that characterize the knowledge economy. Income generated by this sector would be deployed to deal with the unemployment of the unskilled and low-skilled labour, partly in order to reduce the disparity between the incomes of skilled workers and those of the working poor.

It is partly because of these features of action that there has been an increasing search for creative workers. It involves yet another shift in productive orientations. Whereas in industrial economies labour went in search of work, we now find that work increasingly goes in search of labour. Florida (2002) has claimed that what he refers to as the 'creative class', perhaps better conceptualized as a status group, is an important driver of economic growth. According to Follath and Sporl (2007) this 'class' 'is a diverse and colorful group, exemplified by the ability to create ideas that can flow into companies – that will in turn attract return-hungry investors with plenty of start-up capital'. They claim that it is divisible into three groups: 'rational innovators' including engineers, scientists and computer experts; a 'creative middle' such as businessmen, advertising people and designers; and then the 'artists', including musicians, actors and painters. The so-called class is held together less by relations to the means of production or income similarities than by the sharing of a common culture.

Certainly there appears to be broad agreement that the three essential ingredients of a successful knowledge economy are technology, skills and a highly educated labour force (Powell and Snellman, 2004). Increasing human capital is key for innovation and growth. The creative class is claimed to be attracted to locations with open, diverse communities which champion diversity and make cultural creativity accessible. There is general agreement that creativity is increasingly becoming an important part of the economy. Consequently the market value of creative people has risen, and large industries have sought to adapt to how idea-creation assumes ever more importance.

The second determinitive issue is that of globalization. Production in the knowledge economy increasingly targets a global market. This is a consequence of how the regulatory practices of states have declined. Many argue that, as a consequence, the power of the state has also declined. Its interests lie increasingly with global issues and less with the internal socio-economic agenda. The voluntarist and statist discourse gives way to neo-liberalism. It involves a different representation of society and its relationship to the state, while retaining the division between the state, the economic and political power on the one hand, and the frames of social and collective action on the other, with the action of institutions and the individual and collective action lying between them.

When the state dominates the economy, it dominates the public through its imposition of the circumstances in which the individual enters the labour market – language, qualifications, location etc. When this is relaxed and the state involves itself in a globalization of the economy such that economic choice involves more than political decisions, there is a separation of the state from its society. It is argued that the state is there to ensure the welfare of the people, as a benevolent guardian rather than as a leader (Touraine, 2007:45). It is evident in how the EU has moved from its earlier ambitions and moves towards the incorporation of different states, cultures, languages and nations. It is obliged to support a multilingualism and cultural diversity.

It obliges an analysis of systems and an analysis of actors or those who can be considered as subjects. Within industrial society the actor and the system constituted the two faces of the same coin. In the new context, the categories that define the system are totally dissociated from those that define the actor. This means that the form of nationalism that creates a new state as the mirror of the former state no longer applies – it makes collective action redundant. A focus on the state means that social facts are thought of only in terms of the political, and this leads to a sociology without actors and without subjects. It leads to seeing solutions simply in terms of the state and of power (more powers to the Assembly etc.), paying little attention to the people as social actors. Yet the knowledge economy, placing an enhanced importance on human capital, pulls in the opposite direction.

In this paper I would like to explore these developments while asking the question of their implications for language. I will argue that language plays a central role in the knowledge economy and that multilingual working practices can lead to substantial productivity gains for the individual company. This in turn suggests how we need to rethink the nature and value of our own languages. I begin with a consideration of how the social sciences have taken similar realignments in recent years and how this, in turn, accommodates the new understanding of language.

The Social Sciences

All of the social sciences have been subject to considerable ontological reorientation during the past twenty-five years. The two main driving forces of this change have been the strength of post-structuralism and the related awareness of the tacit nature of knowledge. These are aligned with the evident disconnection between theory and empirical research. This leads to substantial changes as the foundational assumptions of Cartesianism are brought into question. This is a concern for disciplines that have tended to have the rationality of the centred human subject at the heart of their theoretical problematics. It results in substantial shifts. In sociology there is a shift away from structure and function, or structure and agency, to a concern with social practice. In economics, the linear, equilibrium models of neo-classical arguments yield to different perspectives, including evolutionary economics and other approaches that focus on the centrality of human capital, and the relationship between social and cultural capital. In Linguistics there is a shift away from a focus on syntax to semantics, and from language to action and discourse. Concepts such as that of 'communication strategies' now involve cultural rather than rational determination, and are increasingly related to how learning by doing insists on a dynamic conception. Psychology is subject to similar refinement, particularly as a consequence of Lacanian and other influences. Thinking is no longer understood as a mechanical process conducted according to procedural programmes, rules or instructions, but involves considerable emphasis on flexibility. Such notions as identity, attitudes or motivation are no longer understood as the effects of determinants of the centred, rational human subject, but as part of the transformation of the individual into the subject of discourse (Williams, 1999). In a sense language and the objects of the social sciences converge.

The social sciences emerged at the same time as the modern state and were very much a product of Cartesian thinking. Furthermore, there is a direct relationship between the state and the concepts of the social sciences. Thus, each state had a single society, a single economy and a single state language and culture. The relationship between language and culture and the state was one in which education was to foster a coherent and unified culture, expressed through a single language in order to foment a unified citizenry. Similarly, the state regulated its economy in order to control the labour market and, in so far as was possible, to ensure full employment and the welfare of the citizenry. This interpretation makes it difficult to avoid thinking of the social sciences and their concepts as the ideological edifice of the state. On the other hand they can be conceived as the elaboration of the concept that make the analysis of the state, its economy and its society possible. What is perhaps more relevant is that when the role of the state declines through globalization and the development of supra-state political-economic institutions, it throws the relationship between key concepts and the framework for these concepts into disarray. Does the society pertain to the state or the European Union? Is the normative system whereby ethnicity is defined by deviation from the normative order a European or a state dimension? Such questions are in abundance and represent a real crisis for the social sciences.

1 Sociology

Where the main criticism of sociology has fallen is on the kind of work that strives to elaborate substantive theories that develop new theories and validate them through empirical observation. It is argued that the elaboration of conceptual tools and the ignoring of the voluntaristic forms of social life has led to a reified, positivistic and often teleological account of social behaviour.

Developments in sociology during the 1980s and 1990s are directly associated with this critique of structure and agency. The rejection of the equilibrium model of social change feeds directly into the conception of structure as a constantly changing entity, so that it is not possible to claim that there can be any direct relationship between structure and agency. Stability only exists as traces of prior discourse, thereby becoming institutions. Furthermore, a static understanding of society such as that which is implicit in the language shift/maintenance dualism becomes totally untenable. Secondly, the individual influences structure in the sense that he or she feeds into the constant changing nature of social structure.

The change in emphasis from patterned human behaviour to social practice, that is, from structure to practice, is central to these developments. While there may well be a structure to behaviour in the sense that it is patterned, this does not help in understanding the relationship between the individual, the subject and behaviour, partly because of the tendency to relate individual behaviour to the structure of which it is part. Social practice relates more to the notion of patterned behaviour as normative. That is, it relates to an understanding of society as consisting of patterns of behaviour that are constantly changing or shifting, but which do so within the context of the capacity to persist as normative for that particular society. We shift from an awareness of structure as something that exists and persists, to one in which it is dynamic, constantly changing and yet persisting as a structure. It is from the issues of social structure and normativity that the notion of social order derives.

Social practice is no longer understood as the product of rationalism, nor as the correlate of a relatively static social structure (Giddens, 1994). The actions of social actors are understood as a continuous flow of conduct which, to the extent that they acquire a certain regularity, takes the form of a social practice. Thus in interaction, while the absence of a subject may well be understood, it does not insist on resorting to models that rely on language, culture, social roles or power as the determining factors. Rather, the pervasive normativity of social life operates by reference to unconscious parameters. Communication always arises in specific contexts and is tied to everyday social practice.

There are at least two fundamental approaches to such issues. On the one hand we have the post-structuralist argument that refutes any role for the centred, rational, human subject. On the other hand sociologists such as Giddens (1984), Bhaskar (1989) and Bourdieu (1987) retain some faith in agency and structure, retaining an ontological view of the individual as a knowledgeable, autonomous agent who is active in formulating his/her action. This is achieved without denying the tacit nature of knowledge. Giddens's theory of structuration shifts the focus from a concern with how structure determines action, to how action is structured as everyday life, and how structured action or social practice is reproduced.

Post-structuralism represents an alternative to Enlightenment materialism, with its focus upon the centred, rational human subject as the source of all meaning (Williams, 1999). It rejects either the subject or reason as the starting-point for social, cultural or political analysis, arguing that both are constructed in and through the discursive process. Furthermore, post-structuralism places stress on the instability and contingency of the structural context of social interaction. This has particular significance for the relationship between the signifier and the signified, in that the notion of a fixed relationship between them is broken. The sign lacks unity, with the infinite play of meaning breaking that unity, and underlining the essential ambiguity of language and meaning.

2 Linguistics

The preoccupation of linguistics has been with form rather than meaning, with syntax rather than semantics. Since Saussure's demarcation of the boundaries of *la langue*, linguists have operated on a pre-constructed object in elaborating their theories of language. That is, the 'language' which they refer to is an object that has been worked on by the state in its various operations of standardization as a form of language planning. As such it sanctions the legitimation of a specific form and, to this extent, syntax is political. This standardization applied not simply to the standard form of a state language, but also to the relationship between different languages within the same state, albeit that the vindication was even more explicit and fierce. It involved the ideal language of grammar and linguistics. It should be evident that all formalist linguistics revolves around a paradigm of analysis that is of little value to the kinds of processes and analyses referred to above.

General grammar focused on what was common to all languages, leading to the science of the laws of language to which all languages are submitted. This defence of universality and the assertion that some categories exist identically in all languages are far removed from a concern with the use of the language and its relationship to the construction of meaning. The object of comparative linguistics was to establish links between specific languages, leading to an emphasis on the kinship analogy of Indo-Europeanism with its particular form of Eurocentrism and even racism. Linguistics sought to distance itself from the explicit political concern of the comparativists and neogrammarians by claiming a concern with the elements of language and a focus on syntax. It was firmly tied to Cartesian rationalism. Thus Chomsky's logico-formalism relies on the competence of the rational human subject as speaker who selects what reflects a norm or sustains a particular model of competence from among a series of possibilities.

This contributed to an awareness that the process leading to describing and using a language is based on the technologies that are the basis of metalinguistic knowledge – the grammar and the dictionary (Auroux,1994). It is never based on the totality of language but on selected representation. It has independence vis-à-vis theory in that it rests on language before there is a meta-language. The idea of languages as homogeneous, always identical to themselves, independent of space, circumstances and speaker, is a consequence of this emphasis. Different languages are characterized by reference to grammatical principles that are not reducible to discursive means, to signification; each language has an autonomous grammatical space. As objects that are analysed according to an internal structure, languages can be compared without reference to signification.

The impact of the Prague School on structural linguistics led to conscious phenomena giving way to the study of their unconscious infrastructure. It was this development that fed into post-structuralism, heralding an awareness that language practice was other than the pure rationalism of Cartesian models. It linked with the influence of Saussure on the social nature of language through how he conceived of *la langue* as a structure of communication that focuses on *parole*. The notion of language as a relatively static form, stabilized by standardization and language purity, gave way to far more dynamic conceptions of language and less of a dogmatic valuation of language forms. An awareness of the essentially ambiguous nature of language opened the door to a much broader range of theorists from Wittgenstein to Bakhtin. It was indicative of a heightened awareness of the importance of semantics and a willingness to treat semantics as extending beyond the essentially narrow constraints of linguistics. It heralded an engagement with discourse.

The diachronic perspective gave way to synchronic analysis and for many the focus also shifts from standard language to what is called natural language. While much of pragmatics persists with the rationalism of the centred subject, this also is changing. It also involves a shift from form to substance, from the rules of standard language to the contents of use. This obliges an engagement with society since how discourses and discursive practices articulate in social space is incapable of being understood simply by resorting to linguistic rules and principles. However, the social is often seen as malleable, as constantly shifting, with the relationship between social practice and institutional organization being particularly problematic.

Language differs from discourse, and the two involve different approaches to linguistics. Language focuses upon the structure or organization of a particular language, and is studied through the application of different models which treat the same linguistic phenomena differently, primarily by emphasizing specific elements or processes. On the other hand discourse pertains to the social and subjective play of 'enunciation'. Given the refutation of the rational subject, the focus is on how the infinite possibilities of language are transposed into meaning as the effects of discourse. The focus is on the social construction of meaning without recourse to the centred subject in the explanation of that construction.

3 Economics

Much like linguistics, the precepts of the neo-classical theory of economics purport to be universal. They rely on the notion of utility maximizing, individual agents who rationally calculate costs and benefits. Much of the criticisms aimed at neo-classical theories of the economy target its failure to establish a convincing framework for understanding some key features of economic systems. This criticism targets two limitations: firstly, how neo-classical economics is blind to what some regard as key aspects of economic behaviour; and secondly, the impact of the new technology on the principals of neo-classicism.

To some extent, neo-classical economics is being replaced by the political conservatism of Hayek and Schumpeter (Hodgson, 1999). Hayek had argued against the capacity of pseudo-market models for innovation as well as the limited view of the central role of knowledge. He claimed that they depicted 'economic man' as 'a quasi-omniscient individual' (1948:33), this leading to ignoring the question of how knowledge was generated and communicated. He also took the equilibrium model to task for inadequately considering knowledge and learning. An awareness of the tacit nature of knowledge undermined the reliance on rationalist conceptions. Yet another issue that was inadequately handled by the neo-classical model was that of trust and cooperation, regarded as essential components of a market economy, and how trust and cooperation are meant to derive from shared values, and thereby from cultural factors. The collectivity assumes a new importance. This undermines the emphasis on the individual agency in neo-classical theory.

The new technology has also led to strong criticism (Quah, 1999). First, it is argued that the process of globalization reduces the state's capacity to intervene in its economic activity, and thereby in its ability to promote equilibrium. The consequence is a far greater diversity, in both the state economy and the global economy. Second, the speed of transactions in an economy which conducts many of its activities electronically gives rise to instability and fluctuation, something that is enhanced by a constant return to scale, path dependency and non-linear pricing. That is, the economy is destabilized by the setting of prices according to new parameters, and the limitation that is placed on entering markets by previous economic history. Finally, the earlier emphasis on how the consumer relies on rationality in making economic decisions gives way to a picture of consumers as constantly learning and reflecting on their circumstances in reaching such decisions. Their actions become much less predictable, and how the economy develops will depend upon the degree of learning, and of knowledge accumulation in operation. This influences markets, which no longer depend on providing the individual consumer with perfect information on the basis of which he/she can make his/her choice. It means that the best strategy for the producer is to generate a diversity of products to meet a constantly changing consumer need.

There is also a rejection of the optimization principles of neo-classical economics which, it is claimed, are unable to account for innovation and technological change because of the tendency to treat them as external to utility maximization. Where emphasis is placed on the importance of interaction involving trust, reciprocity and mutual understanding for an economy where knowledge is of paramount importance, we find the claim that non-optimal economic behaviour should not be seen as irrational, but should be contextualized in order to understand its existence. Thus evolutionary economics is contrasted with modernist regional development theory in emphasizing the particular over the universal (Nelson and Winter,

1982). It stresses the importance of environmental, institutional and cultural differences in how economies evolve. Hayek's distinction between rules and the action that they generate informs how he posits an evolutionism based on a system of rules.

Again we are encountering a shift away from rationalism towards conceptions which focus on the social. Increasingly the tendency to understand the normative practice that constitutes economic behaviour as being constituted by the social and the cultural leads to an emphasis on social practice.

Language use as social practice

These developments raise the question of how we understand language use as social practice. We are here discussing a particular understanding of the nature of language, one that departs from the conventional understanding. It involves how the thread of discourse constructs subjects by transforming the individual into the subject of discourse, and places them in relation to other subjects as well as to objects. I have already maintained that this process is not the rational process of orthodox linguistics and sociolinguistics. Neither is language conceived of as an object, nor as a form, but as a practice. The item of analysis is natural language and how it constitutes an innate talent that is exploited as social practice.

This brings the focus firmly on to discourse. The sociological understanding of self-understanding as conditioned by social practice, and how the individual is transformed into the subject of the associated discourse lends itself well to linguistic approaches that focus upon specific conceptions of discourse (Williams, 1999) and speech action (Bührig, 2003; Bührig and ten Thije, 2008). The rejection of the notion of a linguistic system as a closed and centred totality has generated a renewed interest in discourse, or how the thread of language involves a series of signifying sequences which, when taken together, constitute a more or less coherent framework that conditions what can be said. This notion of discourse breaks with the distinction between thought and reality of orthodox linguistics and most sociolinguistics. It is replaced by the idea of language use as social practice, with most knowledge involving the participants, being tacit. In this respect it also negates the distinction between language and the social, making the linguistic coextensive with the social.

This is not to imply that linguistics and discourse involve the same approach by reference to the play of language. Linguistics pertains to the organization or structure of any particular language, and is studied by reference to different models that treat the same linguistic phenomena differently, often focusing on specific elements or processes. Discourse, on the other hand, involves the subjective and social play of *enonciation* or statement. That is, discourse is a consideration of the utterance from the standpoint of the discursive mechanism that conditions it. It is important to note here that the focus is on the production of a statement. Thus Foucault's (1966) reference to '*énonciative* modalities' does not refer to a propositional content, but to the status and institutional setting of a statement. Discourse does not pertain to the same properties of language as those that are of relevance to the linguist.

To produce or to recognize an utterance is to reconstruct patterns of markers viewed as the traces of operations to which we have no access. In this sense the markers are representative of the inaccessible operations. These are encoded through metalinguistic representation, or the representation of language. Culioli (1976) argues that the patterning of language markers constitutes a form, while referring to the unconscious knowledge of language, and of the nature of language which all speakers have, as epilinguistic. Since we do not control epilinguistic activity, the unconscious nature of epilinguistic knowledge is not presented by the speaker in representation. Linguistic knowledge – the metalinguistic – is represented, constructed and manipulated in the aid of a metalanguage. Since this pertains mainly to the social and the cultural, it is only to a limited extent that this is an individual phenomenon[1].

However, in differing between language and discourse, the argument proceeds to recognizing a form that takes as its object the manifestation of language in living communication – the description of marks and discursive functioning, and their placing in relation to the empirical subjects in different institutional and situational contexts. This establishes the difference between natural language and the language that is described in linguistic terms, the second of which is treated as an artificial language. Culioli (1976) states: 'language is an activity which supposes itself as a perpetual epilinguistic activity.' There is a concern here with an implicit theorization, as well as with how speaking subjects are involved in relation to a 'reflection organizer on the language'. It is something that constantly appears in how the foreign-language learner suspends reference to theory in accessing conceptions related to the acquisition of the mother tongue.

Language and the Subject

This brings us to how the individual becomes the subject of discourse. Within the structural functional framework of twentieth-century sociology, there was a tendency for the individual to be constructed as the outcome of his/her position within the social structure, leading to Garfinkel's (1967) criticism of this notion of the individual as a 'judgemental dope'. The subject is often interpreted in terms of the individual as the creator of him/herself. Evidently this is undermined in theories of discourse.

There is a difference between the individual and the subject of discourse. The human subject comes into being when the individual occupies a particular subject position that opens up in discourse. This subject position bears particular relations to other subject positions as well as to specific objects. Consequently, these relationships play a role in determining what can and must be said from particular subject positions, and it is such structures that determine the action of the individual.

The account of the relationship between the individual and the subject involves attention to interpolation and taking in charge. Taking in charge involves how the subject of *énonciation* is 'supposed to take responsibility for the contents posed', or becomes 'the subject who takes up a position' (Pêcheux, 1982:156). The central thrust of the process focuses on how the individual is constituted as a subject. This occurs through the relationship between interpolation, signification and the taking in charge of discourse. This in turn implies an overlap between a language act that is supported by the construction of meaning, and the *énonciateur* who takes the discourse in charge. The taking in charge derives from the marks in discourse, and how they pertain to the various deictic markers, which set out the range of a field with specific boundaries. Both the act and the event involve the relationship between signification and the real effect, and how the *énonciateur* is transformed into the *locuteur*, occupying a real social place. The formal apparatus of *énonciation* operates when *locuteurs* are taken in charge, implying a social interaction premised upon shared meaning and the implications of a relationship between the *énoncé* and the situation. The individual becomes the subject of discourse. The subject place opens up for the individual to take in charge, or to refuse to take in charge. If someone shouts 'Hey Taff' and I respond, I then become the subject of that discourse, assuming a particular subject place as 'Taff', as the discourse unwinds.

When the individual takes in charge the discourse, that individual is interpolated as the subject of that discourse. This subject is related to other subjects and various objects in such a way that it conditions what can and must be said from the subject place. The discursive activity puts the conventions that regulate the relations between subjects to work, attributing a status to each one. The *énonciateur* is obliged to suppose that the *co-énonciateur* shares all the presuppositions with him/her, in a kind of tacit contract. This notion of place implies that in taking in charge, the individual assumes a subject place, the place of *énonciation*, but simultaneously assigns a complementary place to the 'other' or the *co-énonciateur*. These places support the discourse. Foucault (1969:126) expressed this as 'To describe a formulation while the *énoncé* does not consist of analysing the relations between the author and that which he has said (or wanted to say, or said without wanting to); but to determine what is the position which all individuals can and should occupy in being the subject'.

In a sense, the taking in charge of a discourse confirms an identity in that the individual is interpolated into a subject position that is confirmed and contextualized by reference to other related subjects and objects. Each one accedes to his identity beginning from, and at the interior of, a system of places. In this respect it is important to recognize that the theory of discourse is not a theory of the subject in advance of its constitution through *énonciation*, but rather, it is a theory of the instance of *énonciation* which is, intrinsically and simultaneously, an effect of the *énoncé*. Social identities are constructed within the relationship system of a particular language. In a sense identity is imposed on the individual as subject, and is no longer conceived of through the conscious rationalism implied in a statement such as 'I feel Welsh, therefore I am Welsh.'

The taking in charge of discourse not only transforms the individual into the subject of discourse, but also anchors the subject in relationship to other subjects, and to a range of objects within the discourse. This has profound implications for what can be said, as well as for the legitimacy of what is said. It involves Foucault's notion of *énonciative* modalities as a type of discursive activity that carries its own subject position. In relating *énonciative* modalities to how statements are made, he was emphasizing how discourse is a practice. Social practice is conceived of in terms of discourse relations. The normative now becomes the modality of the object that affords truth value to particular objects

Work in the Knowledge Economy

Having established how language use is conceived of as a form of social practice and how the subject is constructed and constituted in and through discourse, we can now proceed to a consideration of how this relates to a kind of economy that relies heavily on the tacit nature of knowledge. As we shall see, it involves developing the means whereby the individual engages with economic practices as forms of social practice by becoming a subject in relationship to other subjects and different kinds of objects. I begin by elaborating on the importance of language within the production process.

Industrial-age production was characterized by the assembly line, a form of production referred to as Fordism or Taylorism. Different tasks were allocated to different workers who worked independently of one another on the assembly line. Labour activity was mute in the sense that it proceeded without recourse to the use of language. As such, it involved a sense of finitude involving the focus on the end product. This changes profoundly in the knowledge economy. The emphasis shifts from fiscal capital to human capital, from assembly to creativity. Innovation drives productivity, with firms being obliged to enter the market with new products, the notion of 'first to market' being of central importance. Digitization restructures the organization of production; for example, media is transformed into multimedia, and previously separate activities such as film, print, and other forms of media and the different working practices associated with them are merged into a single operation (Williams, 2007). This obliges firms to merge, changing their internal operations. New workflows are brought into existence and the productive activity now focuses on team working within the value chain. This links with an enhanced emphasis on flexibility, and contributes to a reduction in the overriding emphasis on supervision and control, factors that influenced the perceived need to operate within a language that management could understand. Sameness is in decline and self-control is optimized.

The work process in the knowledge economy has tended to be conceptualized by reference to the notion of communities of practice (Wenger, 1997). This largely derives from an awareness that knowledge is tacit in nature. This of course means that since we 'know more than we can say' it is not possible to transfer this knowledge from one person to the other. However, what we know exists in our social practice which leads to the focus on 'learning by doing' wherein workers learn by integrating into the social practice of their co-workers. They learn by observing and reflecting on the working operations of their co-workers, by imitating and by elaborating processes until they become part of their own social practice. Labour is interaction.

In a sense this learning process within communities of practice can be understood as a complex of linguistic and semiotic acts. Integration into the community of practice, accommodating the co-operative process, and the ability to operate seamlessly within it rely upon sharing meaning with other members. This is the *sine qua non* of communities of practice. Evidently the focus is on language as an essential component of work. However, it is not any feature of language. The focus is very much on semantics as opposed to syntax.

This brings the focus on to Bakhtin's (1981) dialogism, Wittgenstein's (1988) language play and Foucault's (1969) discursive practice.

Language and Work

All of this constitutes a profound shift from when economy was identified as the domain of reason, contrasting with the emotional nature of language and culture. This conception resulted in constraints on the use of minority languages which had to remain outside the world of reason. Consequently, the minority-language speaker could only be accepted as *homo economicus* while operating through the language of reason, the state language. It was the outcome of Cartesianism and its role in subverting the former political order. It involved an overriding concern with civilization and barbarism, the very discourse whose institutionalized traces make all of us racists. It also involved what Deleuze (Lecercle, 2002) has called the society of control by reference to language. It was a discourse that had profound influences on the social sciences as meta-discourses. It has taken the undermining of Cartesianism to offer a release from such constraints on language and culture.

The essential question I wish to highlight involves the extent to which the generation of knowledge benefits from working across language and culture. Does multilingualism have an inherent productive advantage? Labour based on communication and on the centrality of language for communication does not possess a rigid finalistic structure. That is, it is not determined by a predetermined objective, but rather, involves an ongoing process of exploration and discovery. This is on account of the entirely ambiguous nature of language, with language being capable of generating an infinite body of knowledge and meaning. That is, language is an inherently creative medium. In a sense we can conceive of labour based on communication as an activity devoid of work. We also recognize that there is an overlap between the rules of a project and those of its execution, such that they are one and the same. There is no distinction between intention and realization.

Marx's (1906) focus on how a 'product is inseparable from the act of producing' involves activities that are not objectified in a lasting product. Arendt (1958) points out that what I refer to as 'activity without work' shares a great deal in common with politics. Creative workers – artists, dancers, actors, musicians etc. – require a public in order to demonstrate their virtuosity, much in the same way as politicians require an electorate. Thus labour within the knowledge economy demands attitudes and characteristics similar to those of political praxis – open presentation to others, the management of degrees of unpredictability, the ability to begin new projects, and the ability to negotiate alternative possibilities. The last feature is the essence of a reflexive practice that constantly asks, 'Why are things done the way they are, and what alternative ways are possible?'

While acceptance of the link between creativity and the essentially ambiguous nature of language lays claim to the value of language for knowledge generation, we still need to consider how this is operationalized. Questions of reflexivity are raised once the relationship between language and the world is not simply one of direct representation. Furthermore, reflexivity as a form of self-awareness is problematized once one maintains that the individual becomes a subject only in and through discourse. These two observations condition how reflexivity is reassessed in relation to tacit knowledge. The rationality of behaviour implies a reflexive activity.

There is no suggestion that the social actors are in control and determine the thread of discourse in its entirety. It is clearly impossible for any actor to be fully in charge of any discourse, as a consequence of which rationality is not only clearly limited, but is also reflexive. When we consider reflexivity as the interpretative capacity of the producers of meaning we are, somehow, able to create distinctive forms of meaning for language objects. The essential ambiguity of meaning, and how meaning is manifested in the discursive formation and the materiality of language, is the key to reflexivity. The signifier–referent relation only exists within and through discourse. Most importantly creativity rests in reflexive practice.

The problem is succinctly put by Authier (1995:803) who claims that once one accepts that the process of *énonciation* is not transparent to the *énonciateur*, one has ceased to 'believe in taking the *énonciateurs* at their word'. That is, it is not possible to consider the images involved in a statement as expressing a faithful mirror, giving direct access to the object. In order to comprehend the status of these forms of auto-representation in the *énonciative* process where they operate, it is again necessary to explore beyond that which they represent. They represent traces of a 'negotiation', inherent to the *énonciation*, but which is also something that cannot be represented.

There are several forms of linguistic knowledge, or knowledges of language. In speaking we all claim to 'know' the language we use in one way or another. We always tend to relate knowledge to the conscious and the reflexive – in order to know, it is necessary that one knows what one knows! Culioli (1968:40) claimed that language rests on 'non-conscious linguistic activity'. It is an activity that is in no way controlled. This means that while we may believe that reflexivity is a conscious process, we are not aware either of the tools that we use, nor the processes wherein those tools operate. The subject's reflection on his/her own language activity, according to Culioli, varies by culture, and involves differences conditioned by language. Culture, as well as the social, is incorporated into language practice. Thus reflexive activity is something that varies across languages. He outlines the relationship between properties of language and the reflexive process.

Considering the relevance of discourse with a focus on ambiguity inevitably leads to a consideration of the relationship between the subject and the production of meaning as something that is produced in interaction. This process of reflexivity in language is enhanced when the interaction involves more than one language. If we follow Culioli in accepting that the socio-cultural is an essential feature of how meaning is constituted in and through interaction, we also recognize the existence of distinctive reflexive processes for each language object. Herein lies the value of linguistic diversity for the generation of knowledge, and indeed, for creativity. The reflexivity partly relates to the relation between language components and signification, something that is subject to considerable variation. This involves an awareness of how translating language is relatively easy, whereas the translation of meaning is of quite a different order. Meaning must be constantly contextualized, and when this occurs across languages, the nature of reflexivity is intensified. If this is indeed correct, then it would appear that the value of working within communities of practice which operate across languages would be far more productive by reference to the generation of both knowledge and innovation than operating within monolingual contexts. Thus, rather than pragmatically seeking to stimulate the flow of operations by insisting on the use of a common lingua franca, firms would be much better off if they facilitated linguistic diversity in their operations.

This is not unrelated to how Nonaka (1994) refers to the development of a model of 'organizational model creation'. He argues that if knowledge-based organizations wish to transform individual implicit knowledge into explicit knowledge, they must pursue intensive communication processes such as 'rounds of meaningful dialogues', or the use of metaphors, which may give individuals an insight into their implicit knowledge (Nonaka, 1994). His model of knowledge conversion (Nonaka and Takeuchi, 1995) involves the following stages:

(1) socialisation, involving how individual tacit or implicit knowledge is transferred into collective tacit knowledge. This builds on sharing practical examples, common experiences and physical proximity;
(2) externalisation, transforms this collective tacit or implicit knowledge into collective explicit knowledge (from embedded to encoded knowledge). This is essential in developing a common basis for sharing tacit knowledge;
(3) combination, which, in converting knowledge, generates individual explicit knowledge out of collective explicit knowledge. The already explicitly expressed components of (collective) knowledge are systematically transformed into a new combination, thus producing a new form of knowledge;

(4) internalisation, as the final stage of knowledge creation, transforms individual explicit knowledge into individual tacit knowledge. It involves personal interaction, applying the new knowledge in practice-oriented situations and a high level of involvement.

Evidently, if these processes involve the use of more than one language there will be an enhanced reflective process in operation, a process which involves not merely metaphors, but also the entire range of discursive functions which involves signification and the symbolic, as they relate to the construction of the relationships between subjects and objects. These are the essential ingredients of shared meaning that transcends both language and culture. However, the essential point made here is that creativity is as much a process as it is an event.

Research on knowledge-sharing and innovation culture tends to emphasize learning by doing, which involves iterative, trial-and-error interactive feedback from experimentation by actors to survive and prosper economically. The greater the variety, the greater the opportunity for innovation arising from interactions with other actors. Opportunities for the swiftest innovation occur in conditions of proximate and related variety (Boschma 2005). This is the essence of the notion of communities of practice, and operating such systems across language and culture promotes the kind of reflexive learning that is essential for innovation and knowledge generation.

These views on language and social practice are at odds with those views that claim a relationship between perception and behaviour, which separate the mind from speech as behaviour. They also raise questions about the relationship between language and culture. That there is a relationship between them is clear. However, we would be reluctant to claim that 'language reflects culture', or involves 'turning thoughts into words'. This assumes a particular understanding of language, one that is removed from language and social practice. It is possible to learn a language without also learning the culture. Social practice relies on both language and culture, and communicative competence implies a simultaneous mastering of both. Similarly, the perspective outlined above equates words and thought, rather than treating them as separate qualities. It also questions assumptions about language as a 'reference framework', with each framework serving as the conduit for different 'perspectives'. Sufficient has been said above about the difference between language and discourse, and about the limitations of rationalism, for this to be self-evident.

Our understanding of the dynamic nature of culture, and the role of language in this dynamism, is expressed by Carter (2004:78): 'Speakers transmit, reproduce, modify, transgress and continually remake the cultures they inhabit by means of their ordinary speech ... Speakers are social actors and agents of culture, and are transitive in their encounters, shaping and reshaping their language in ways which encode that how they mean is a significant component in what cultures mean and what people mean as speakers within their cultures.' That is, culture is not a fixed inheritance from the past that is somehow divorced from daily life, but relates to identities between people and the social institutions to which they relate.

Implications for the Welsh Language

In discussing the implications of the above conception, I would like to focus upon three issues – education, language planning and the economy.

1 Education

Wales suffers from the same malaise in terms of language learning as does England. The fact that Wales is supposedly a bilingual nation makes no apparent difference to the limited desire on the part of Welsh people to become multilingual. Currently, this leaves the UK and Ireland as the worst states in terms of language learning (Williams et al. 2007). This partly relates to the perceived difficulty of language learning and partly to the misunderstanding which maintains that a knowledge of English is sufficient in the global knowledge economy. Significantly it also leaves the teaching of Welsh as the only successful teaching of non-mother tongue languages in the UK. There is a great deal that can be learnt from this success and this advantage should be strategically exploited.

Clearly the preceding discussion implies that there is a reassessment of the nature of language and of its role in the economy. Given that a primary function of education is to provide the labour for the economy, this has to be taken into account in the planning of language learning. The starting-point for such a development is again the centrality of social practice. The goal is that of allowing the learner to communicate, not necessarily in terms of any sense of language purity, but rather, in terms of the generation of meaning. This has to occur in contexts of multilingual language use as social practice. This is achieved to a high level of competence in teaching Welsh in Welsh-medium schools, but is abysmal to the teaching of other languages. What is missing in terms of mastering Welsh is the confidence to use the competence.

It also means a retreat from the teaching of languages in terms of syntax, and a shift to a concern with semantics and their operation. The conventions whereby meaning is operationalized should be taught by reference to factors other than an idealized form of syntax. We must place far less emphasis on language purity and the 'correct' forms of oral and written expression. Rather, the focus should be on the colloquial forms that will allow communication to operate and meaning to be shared. Given that with Welsh we are in the throes of establishing a new form of linguistic normativity, this may not be easy.

By the same token, the teaching of high culture, whether it involves literature, art, architecture, or some other form, is no longer of relevance. This does not mean that culture should not be targeted in education. The desired level of communication will be thwarted unless knowledge of language is accompanied by an immersion in the associated culture. Here we are not referring to the forms of high culture but to those which we draw on in operationalizing social practice. Insofar as is possible, there should be an integration of cultural aspects as a feature of social practice by integrating the learner into social practice as the subject of the relevant discourse.

The learning of languages should be accompanied by the learning of how to analyse and solve problems as well as providing access to cultural forms of expression. The focus shifts to learning by doing. It also involves striving to emphasize the learning of reflexive practice which, in turn, should lead not only to a reflection on meaning but also on language in relationship to its environment.

The increased argument in favour of beginning language teaching at a young age mirrors Welsh language teaching. In terms of the emphasis on language use as social practice, the importance of this development lies in how the experience of social practice is somewhat more natural at a young age. It should lead to the ability to merge social practices through living them rather than by means of a mechanical transfer from those associated with one language to another. Wherever possible, this should involve using the languages in daily life.

This may involve explaining the relationship between an activity and social practice so that there is an acceptable fit between them. It will involve emphasizing classification of the practice, the associated principles of language and cultural use, and an evaluation of its effectiveness. This invariably leads to matters of choice so that different scenarios and language uses can be evaluated. It involves frequent peer-to-peer practice, something that will also enhance confidence in language use with different social *interlocuteurs*.

2 Language planning

Language planning has to recognize two things. Firstly, it must depart from a preoccupation with the static concepts of language maintenance and language shift. This derives from a framework that is no longer tenable. It must recognise that language and culture are constantly dynamic concepts which affect all languages. This does not mean that there are not points of discursive stability. The problems that derive from a conceptualization of language in terms of maintenance and shift derive from structural functionalism, and from the enormous influence of Fishman's book on *Reversing Language Shift* (Williams, 2007b). This is not to decry the massive contribution made by Fishman to an understanding of language in society, but rather to emphasize that the field now requires a different orientation. By the same token it must abandon concepts such as domain and diglossia, which merely focus on structural aspects of language behaviour.

Secondly, it must do more than think in terms of language objects and focus more on social processes including language use as social practice. That is, language planning relates to much more than a focus on the production and reproduction of language. It must develop a concern with the subject and with language use as social practice. Again it involves rethinking concepts such as that of 'normalization' which tells us little more than that there is a goal or a desire to make the use of a specific language 'normal'. This can be achieved by engaging with normativity in such a way that institutionalization is recognized as social practice. That is, it does not involve centred, rational actors striving to make the use of a language 'normal' within a political engagement. This means that it must discover ways in which the learning of a language involves the learning of the entire repertoire of use contexts in relation to culture such that the emerging social practice occurs with the minimum degree of reflexivity.

Thirdly, it must encompass a new understanding of the relationship between language and the economy. Language use has to focus on the private sector, persuading companies, especially those operating within the knowledge economy, of the value of multilingual and multicultural working practice. There must be an understanding of the knowledge economy and how language plays a key role in that economy. There should be a willingness to encompass training programmes for working across language and cultures within specific workflows. Projects such as Cymru'n Creu should be persuaded of the productive value of the cultural economy and of the role of the media producer in generating multimedia content within the project (Williams, 2003). This will involve redrafting management and organizational structures which should result in the disappearance of key institutions. This may prove difficult, but it is only through such an engagement that the work process can be clearly understood.

What the introduction on the emphasis on human capital within the production process achieves is an understanding of the role of language in relation to the economy as something which everyone benefits from, regardless of their language competences. This is quite different from a context in which the emphasis is placed upon the divisive nature of labour market segmentation, justified by an appeal to a nebulous sense of rights supported by reference to the concept of autochthony. It means that if multilingualism does provide the added value that is claimed in terms of knowledge generation, everyone within a particular economy will benefit. It is also a notion that is much better suited to the context of globalization where value chains and labour markets are extended and migration becomes the rule.

This process also demands clarification of how globalization interferes with the established aims of language planning. Within the global economy, the role of the state is changing. This is not merely a reference to the nature of neo-liberalism, but a realization that when the state dominates the economy, it dominates the public through its imposition of the circumstances within which the individual enters the labour market – language, qualifications, location etc. When this is relaxed and the state involves itself in a globalization of the economy such that economic choice involves more than political decisions, there is a separation of the state from its society. It is evident in how the EU has moved from its earlier ambitions, and towards the incorporation of different states, cultures, languages and nations. It is obliged to support a multilingualism and cultural diversity. This should be grasped by language planners, and there should be a firm involvement with the broader dimensions of multilingualism. It involves abandoning the preoccupation with Welsh as a minority language and a willingness to view it merely as one of several languages confronting the effects of the new economic order. We must stop thinking of ourselves in terms of that which we are not – not English or not European, non-Welsh speakers etc., and construct a more positive conception of self, one that is global in nature and that accords to others that which we may feel is denied to ourselves.

3 The economy

When considering the relevance of language for the economy, we must recognize that this is the main motivating force in terms of a desire to produce and reproduce Welsh. It is evident that currently the relationship between a knowledge of Welsh and the labour market is, by and large, restricted to the public sector, and that it is here that we identify the potential for a relationship between a knowledge of Welsh and social mobility. The private sector must be persuaded of the value of multilingualism for production and profit. This is not a matter of relying upon legislation, but rather, one of creating the context wherein everyone gains from multilingualism, and not merely the bilingual or multilingual population. If it can be seen that language makes a positive contribution to the economy writ large and that the private sector will gain advantage through operating multilingually, we will have turned an important corner.

We still talk about the economy and language as if they were entirely separate activities. Labour markets have changed significantly and the relationship between states, their official languages and labour markets is in flux. States whose languages are not lingua franca experience labour market segmentation, in which well-paid international employment demands a knowledge of one or more of the lingua francas, whereas the domestic labour market demands a knowledge of the state language. This is precisely the kind of relationship experienced by some minority languages in the relationship between space, language and the economy.

One of the few assets that Wales has in the knowledge economy is the creative sector (Cooke, 2006). However it lacks leadership and direction. The process of transforming the media sector into multimedia production is desperately slow, and little attempt seems to have undertaken to attract exploiters of the creative sector (Williams, 2003). In the meantime, media companies are going out of business, partly on account of their own lack of flexibility in the relationship between language and markets. Valuable skills are being lost. Even fewer attempts have been made to blend the advantages of the creative sector with its bilingualism. We seem preoccupied with the false duality of a Welsh-speaking and an English-speaking Wales, each with its sphere of action and relevance.

Distinguishing between the cultural economy and the creative economy allows us to recognize different but related possibilities. The cultural economy has enormous potential. The creation of the cultural archive is well under way, but its commercial exploitation through the creation of a productive sector is not even being considered. Granted that, in all probability, the necessary diversification of cultural assets is insufficiently large to support such a sector on its own, it is still possible for links and partnerships to exploit a European-wide archive by working across language and culture through online, end-to-end, production systems. The global nature of the economy and the new technology allow the targeting of cultural and linguistic diasporas, either alone or in partnership with other nations and cultures. The scope is massive, especially at a time when content is in such short supply.

The creative economy represents a different challenge. Thus far it has been conceived simply in terms of the creative capacity of those working in the key occupations and the fact that there is a tendency for them to cluster in specific locations. The exploitation of the implicit or explicit skills appears to rely on the willingness of firms and capital to target the potential. This obliges a degree of diversification so that the potential that resides in the new technology workers can work side by side with the creative workers. There is little doubt that the creative potential of language is one dimension that would contribute significant added value to such a context.

Conclusion

In this paper, I have sought to outline the value of language for the new economy while also demonstrating how the orthodox approach to the relationship between language, society, and the economy has changed. I argue that this obliges a reformulation of our understanding of language and of its relevance for our lives. Unfortunately, most of the work thus far undertaken on language and the economy has been orthodox in nature, making interesting claims for the role of language through reconfiguring orthodox economic principles, or by demonstrating how companies which fail to pay attention to language within their marketing practices and strategies fail to work to their potential (CILT, 2006). I argue that this is inadequate, and that what is required is a thorough understanding of how the economy is changing and how language can play a new and profitable role in the new context.

Notes

[1] There is some similarity between this conception of Culioli's and Austin's speech action pattern. However since Austin's pragmatics relies on the centred, rational subject the similarity is perhaps more evident by reference to the work of Bakhtin (1981).

References

Arendt, H. (1958). *The Human Condition*, Chicago, University of Chicago Press.
Auroux S. (1994). *La Revolution technologique de la grammatisation*, Paris, Mardaga.
Authier, J. (1995). *Ces mots qui ne vont pas de soi*, Paris, Larousse, vols 1 and 2.
Bakhtin, M. (1981). *The Dialogical Imagination*, Austin, University of Texas Press.
Bhaskar R. (1989). *Reclaiming Reality*, London, Verso.
Boschma, R.A. (2005). 'Proximity and innovation: a critical assessment', *Regional Studies*, 39, 1, 61–74.
Bourdieu, P. (1987). *Choses Dites*, Paris, Minuit.
Bührig, Kristin (2003). 'Gesundheitsfalle Haushalt: Sprachlich-kommunikative Charakteristika einer Krankenkassenbroschüre', in Jörg Hagemann and Sven F. Sager (eds.), *Schriftliche und mündliche Kommunikation. Festschrift zum 65. Geburtstag für Klaus Brinker*, Tübingen: Stauffenburg, pp. 61–75.
Bührig, Kristin and ten Thije, Jan D. (2008). 'Diskurspragmatische Beschreibung', to appear in Ulrich Ammon, Norbert Dittmar, Klaus Matthaei and Peter Trudgill (eds.), *Soziolinguistik. Sociolinguistics*, HSK 3, 123, Berlin, de Gruyter.
Carter, R. (2004). *Language and Creativity*, London, Routledge.

CILT (2006). *ELAN: Effects on the European Economy of Shortages of Foreign Language Skills in Enterprise*, EC, DGE&C.

Cooke, P. N. (2006). *The Creative Industries in Wales – and Their Discontents*, Gregynog Seminar on Promoting Welsh Creative Industries: Making the Most of Our European Links, January 2006.

Culioli, A. (1968). 'La Formalisation en linguistique', *Cahiers pour l'Analyse*, 9.

Culioli, A. (1976). *Considérations sur un prgramme de traitement automatique des langues et du langage*, Pitfall, 26, University of Paris 7.

Florida, R. (2002). *The Rise of the Creative Class: And How It Is Transforming Work, Leisure, Community and Everyday Life*, New York, Basic Books.

Follath, E. and G. Sporl (2007). 'An inside look at Europe's coolest cities', *Der Spiegel*, 28 August 2007.

Foucault, M. (1966). *Les Mots et les choses*, Paris, Gallimard.

Foucault, M. (1969). *L'Archeologie du savoir*, Paris, Gallimard.

Garfinkel, H. (1967). *Studies in Ethnomethodology*, Englewood Cliffs, Prentice Hall.

Giddens, A. (1984). *The Constitution of Society*, Cambridge, Polity.

Giddens, A. (1994). *Beyond Left and Right: The Future of Radical Politics*, Cambridge, Polity.

Giddens, A. (2002). *Runaway World: How Globalisation is Reshaping our Lives*, London, Profile Books.

Hayek F. A. (1948). *Individualism and Economic Order*, London, Routledge.

Hodgson, G. M. (1999). *Economics and Utopia*, London, Routledge.

Lecercle, J.-J. (2002). *Deleuze and Language*, London, Palgrave.

Marx, K. (1906). *Capital: A Critique of Political Economy*, vol. IV, Chicago, Kerr.

Nelson, R. R. and Winter, S. G. (1982). *An Evolutionary Theory of Economic Change*, Cambridge, Mass, Harvard University Press.

Nonaka, I. (1994). 'A dynamic theory of organizational knowledge creation', *Organization Science*, 5, 1, 14–37.

Nonaka, I. and Takeuchi, H. (1995). *The Knowledge-Creating Company: How Japanese Companies Create the Dynamics of Innovation*, Oxford, Oxford University Press.

Pêcheux, M. (1982). *Language, Semantics and Ideology*, London, Macmillan.

Powell, W. W. and Snellman, K. (2004). 'The knowledge economy', *Annual Review of Sociology*, 30, 199–220.

Quah, D. (1999). *The Weightless Economy in Economic Development*, Working Paper 155, UN University WIDER, Helsinki.

Touraine, A. (2007). 'La Place du sujet', in M. Wieviorka (ed.), *Les Sciences sociales en mutation*, Paris, Éditions Sciences Humaines.

Wenger, E. (1997). *Communities of Practice: Learning, Meaning and Identity*, Cambridge, Cambridge University Press.

Williams, G. (1999). *French Discourse Analysis: The Method of Post-structuralism*, London, Routledge.

—— (2003). TEDIP: Technology, Economics and Diversity in the Periphery, EU IST-1999-20193, Final Report, EC, Luxemburg.
—— (2005). *Sustaining Language Diversity in Europe*, London, Pergamon.
—— (2007a). 'From media to multimedia: workflows and language in the digital economy', in M. Cormack and N. Hourigan (eds.), *Minority Language Media*, Clevedon, Multilingual Matters, pp. 88–107.
—— (2007b). 'Reversing language shift: a sociological visit, *Plurilingua*, 30, 161–79.
Williams, G., Strubell, M., Vilaro Valejo, S. and G. O. Willaims (2007). *The Development of Language Teaching in Europe*, report EAC 28/06 presented to DGEAC, October 2007.
Wittgenstein, L. (1988). *Tractatus Logico-philosophicus*, London, Routledge.

From Act to Action in Wales

Colin H. Williams
School of Welsh
Cardiff University

Introduction

This contribution seeks to tackle the question: To what extent have key aspects of the 1993 Welsh Language Act been effective? The answer is based on evidence gathered over a period of three years which reflects the experience and response of policy-makers, public officials charged with implementing the Act, and those Welsh Language Board staff responsible for regulating the process, dealing with complaints, conducting investigations and submitting advice and recommendations to the government via the minister so as to ensure compliance with the Act.

Currently there is pressure to update and reform the process by which the political and legislative aspects of creating a bilingual Wales, Iaith Pawb's declared aim, can be achieved. Among the proposals discussed there have been calls for a new language act at Westminster, additional linguistic clauses and legislation as part of the National Assembly's commitment to increasing equality and advancing the anti-discrimination agenda (Cymdeithas yr Iaith Gymraeg, 2005). More significantly there has been a government-inspired debate on the abolition or restructuring of the Welsh Language Board. It is anticipated that some of its duties would be subsumed into a Language Commission which would promote the language, develop policies, coordinate government activities in favour of the Welsh language, investigate routine complaints and gather evidence for the formulation of far-reaching policies. There have also been calls for the creation of the post of language commissioner, who would be an independent actor, answerable to the Assembly, and not to a minister within the government. Thus while the commission would promote the language the commissioner would focus on implementation issues. The primary role of the commissioner, as in the Canadian example, would be to ensure that language legislation works, to investigate serious breaches of the legislation and to offer practical and statutory methods by which the outstanding obstacles to bilingual service delivery and the honouring of language rights might be resolved (COL, 2005, 2007). Accompanying these institutional changes there would need to be a clarification and statutory definition of the rights of individuals, whether as customers, employees or students. New legislation would establish specific rights for those domiciled in Wales, such as the right to become fluent in Welsh, and the right to express oneself in Welsh, whether in speech or writing, in dealings with public bodies and some private agencies or companies. These rights would evolve as the system is reformed so as to realize the bilingual character of society and in time to underpin the normative as well as the official standing of Welsh. A related issue would be the rights of Welsh speakers elsewhere in the UK.

Underlying this political, ideological activity and lobbying there are a number of aspirations and expectations which are not always fully articulated. Consequently there is an urgent need to examine to what extent the existing system is satisfactory *in toto,* a task which has not hitherto been attempted. Most of the disquiet expressed is based on partial and idiosyncratic experiences rather than on a comprehensive analysis of how the system works. Thus an essential prerequisite should be the systematic gathering of time-series information related to the various indicators used in monitoring performance. Too often we are tempted to rely on ideology and rhetoric, rather than on sound data. Granted that the philosophical, political and social basis of the movement for the promotion of Welsh is much more complex than is often admitted, it would certainly be unwise to support all the proposals made in favour of the language currently discussed in the media and various interest networks without evaluating the likely impact and full cost of such proposals. Nevertheless it is salutary to ask a number of difficult, if key, questions in order to remind ourselves that informed discussion and analysis is needed so as to modify or temper the more emotional responses which often pass for language policy. The situation is too fragile for us not to engage in careful evaluation and prioritization; for fear that we dissipate our limited energies on minor details and not focus on fundamentals and those structures most conducive to the interests of citizens who wish to see the Welsh language flourish.

Thus we may ask

- What is the purpose of legislation?
- What model of society is envisaged?
- What is the relationship between the individual and the system?
- How do language rights fit with other human rights?
- What is practical and acceptable and to whom?

Evaluating the Effect of Language Legislation: The 1993 Welsh Language Act

In order to attempt an answer some of these questions an evaluation was conducted of the impact of language legislation across Europe and specifically in Finland, Ireland and Wales. This essay focuses only on Wales.[1] The investigation was structured along the following lines: the posing of key questions, the gathering of data from a number of institutions in Wales and other parts of the United Kingdom, the selection of units for in-depth observation work, a critique of the history of certain organizations' involvement with the Act and with the Welsh Language Board in the regulation of language schemes, detailed interviews within a number of bodies, their heads of department, language officers and other officers who were not directly involved with bilingual services, Assembly and Westminster ministers. The results were then compared with similar investigations undertaken in Ireland and Finland so as to produce generic, European examples of best practice and recommendations for systematic legislative and public administrative reform.

The Welsh Language Board was established as a statutory element under the 1993 Act, to promote the Welsh language. In its early phase the board was essentially a grant allocation body steering its partners into certain activities. It also undertook the approval and regulation of Welsh language schemes. Initially the WLB was very conscious that it was involved in statutory intervention in an area where the Welsh language had hitherto been overly dependent on good will alone. In time the board became a recognized language planning body and the main formal, officially sanctioned body influencing language policy in Wales. This structural change was the result of a number of factors, amongst which could be noted: the board's maturity and the increasing experience of its staff and members, a new operating framework and political system following the establishment of the National Assembly for Wales, a substantial increase in the board's funding and in consequence its ability to act and take a leading role in emerging areas, for example, marketing and the private sector. Most critical was the changing nature of the relationship between the WLB and its constituent public as one was less likely to hear accusations that it was an irrelevance, ineffective or as a former quango, a governmental stooge unwittingly involved in the deflection of attention away from the fundamental issue of securing full and free rights for Welsh speakers.

The 1993 Act made it obligatory for institutions in the public sector and justice administration to adopt new ways of treating Welsh and English on an equal basis, mainly through the preparation of statutory Welsh language schemes (HMSO, 1993). Under the Act every organization named by the government was obliged to submit a draft language scheme to the Welsh Language Board for approval as an executive statutory scheme. For the first time statutory regulations undergirded aspects of the public administration and socio-economic life of an increasingly bilingual country.

Welsh Language Schemes

Under the 1993 Language Act language schemes were established as the main means of ensuring a bilingual service within the public sector, while treating both languages on the basis of equality. Section 11 of the Act notes that the Welsh language scheme applies to public bodies (all sectors) and Crown bodies, as well as organizations eligible under the public service remit e.g. water companies. Sections 5–16 concentrate on institutional duties, and on the form, content and process of the preparation, consultation, approval and review of language schemes. Sections 12 and 13 of the Act, specify that it is compulsory for a scheme to note a schedule for action, to offer a description of the manner in which a named body would ensure publicity for its scheme and how it would seek consultation with the public in accordance with the statutory guidance offered by the board. The board maintained the right to review the guidelines and to review the schemes every three years for local authorities and every five years for educational bodies.

A single statutory guideline (Section 9 of the Act) for all public bodies in Wales deals with the following:

- A bilingual scheme
- Approach to service provision (in line with the principle of equality)
- New policies and initiatives
- Steps for the introduction of services
- Quality standards – for Welsh-language services
- Dealing with the Welsh-speaking public
- The public face of the institution
- The implementation and supervision of the scheme.

The supervisory and implementation guidelines contain measures on evaluation and regulation in relation to human resources, language and vocational training, the administration of third-party-agreement schemes, the supervision of the scheme, achieving targets and the publication of information.

Compliance is the basic principle underlying Sections 17–20 where four specific aspects are discussed, namely investigations (Section 17), complaints about non-compliance (Section 18), reports on investigations (Section 19) and directives from the secretary of state (Section 20).

One may wish to question the original intention behind this method of service provision. Why was the language scheme chosen as the tool for changing expectations and behaviour in the public sector, and not, for instance, the recognition and reinforcement of individual language rights? At interview some of the government lawyers who were responsible for drawing up the Language Act, argued that they did not believe that pursuing individual rights would be a productive approach. This was mainly because they believed that there was little or no agreement on the extent of any obligation in law to recognize the precise nature of individual rights. They were acutely conscious of several strategic changes in the field of international language legislation stemming from the United Nations declaration in 1948 which stated:

> Everyone is entitled to all the rights and freedoms set forth in this Declaration, without distinction of any kind, such as race, colour, sex,

> language, religion, political or other opinion, national or social origin, property, birth or other status. (Universal Declaration of Human Rights 1948, Article 2)
>
> Everyone has the right to education. Education shall be free, at least in the elementary and fundamental stages. Elementary education shall be compulsory. Technical and professional education shall be made generally available and higher education shall be equally accessible to all on the basis of merit. (Article 26)

It was also recognized that numerous other proposals have been made since then. Thus the decision not to focus on a rights-based approach could not be attributed either to a lack of awareness or a lack of understanding of this area, but rather to the pressing political desire to provide a bilingual service in response to the long period of campaigning for bilingual forms, signage and so on. The justification given for the language schemes was that they represented an instrumental means of securing public recognition that Welsh could be an appropriate language for public administration and local government. Elsewhere I have critiqued this decision and offered an analysis of the weaknesses of current legislation as regards the Welsh language (Williams, 2005, 2007b). Here I want to acknowledge one basic fact. Despite the Welsh lack of commitment to individual rights, it is evident from observations and interviews conducted in relation to international perspectives on language legislation, that a number of regulatory systems, such as those of Canada and Finland, regret the fact that they do not have anything similar to language schemes in place. Several times in interviews with senior officials in the Canadian federal government or with High Court judges, they alluded to the advantages of language schemes as a way of ensuring a bilingual service that was continually evolving and capable of being monitored in a routine fashion.

In the Irish case, based to some extent on the 1993 Welsh Language Act, when the Official Languages Act was passed in 2003, the responsibility to offer a service was combined with the right to receive a service. The Act places specific duties on public bodies and also establishes the public's basic rights to receive public services through the medium of the Irish language. The Act enables the government to require public-sector bodies to draw up language schemes based on the Welsh experience. Currently there are approximately 900 official or semi-official bodies in existence, and of these a small number have already been notified under Section 9 of the Act of their obligation to draw up and implement a language scheme. In future it will be possible to extend the reach of the Act to encompass other sectors, such as energy providers, banks and insurance and telecommunications companies. As well as outlining arrangements for the provision of services to the public through the medium of Irish, the schemes also deal with the internal use made by organizations of Irish. It is a requirement of all public-organization offices in the Gaeltacht that they conduct their administration through the medium of Irish, and the government has the power to set up a fund to compensate individuals who do not receive services in the Irish language.

In order to safeguard rights and evaluate to what extent language schemes fulfil their obligations, the 2003 Act set up an Official Languages Commission. The commissioner, Seán Ó Cuirreáin, has the power to consider complaints, conduct investigations and take legal action against any organization that fails to provide the information requested. As well as submitting a complaint to the commissioner, individuals can use the courts to secure their rights.

In Wales the Welsh Language Board guides the process of agreeing on a scheme once the minister has named an organization under the Language Act. Consequently the board's conduct is crucial to the success of the process and thus the way it deals with language schemes from day to day is significant. The chief executive and chair of the board granted their unconditional permission for this current investigation to examine the process in detail. This enabled me to read every file and follow up all cases that were of interest to the project. It also allowed me to work at the board's offices several times a week for a period of fourteen months, during which time I examined documents, decisions and the processes by which board's officials dealt with and investigated complaints and how they discussed routine issues. This freedom to ask questions and to record the main features of the WLB's professional working methods was invaluable. A number of opportunities were granted to interview the chief executive; heads of units and board officers, and all data requested were made available. Board staff who supervise the schemes were ready to give advice not only on their actions but also on their views as to how the process could be improved. Similarly when interviews were conducted with local government representatives, Crown body and central government offices, full cooperation was forthcoming, as was a frank discussion concerning their views on their dealings with board officials and other agencies.

Key Questions

In each institution visited questions were asked about seven elements which were likely to affect the quality and nature of the bilingual service provided. In this chapter only material concerned with language schemes will be discussed in detail. The seven elements were as follows:

- The scope of the Language Act(s)
- National supervision methods
- Implementation of the language scheme
- Supervision of the language scheme
- The range of services
- Do the language schemes work?
- What improvements are needed?

During 2005–7, when the research was conducted, there were about 350 language schemes in place. Today over 534 are in existence. The introduction of Welsh-language schemes heralded a new way of treating Welsh as an integral element of public administration. The Act has introduced a language policy which included a commitment to serve the public, and this became standard practice in the wake of language schemes Consequently an important element of this investigation was an evaluation of the professional climate in which schemes operated. Clearly the organizational culture within which the duty to prepare a bilingual service is handled is vital, since attitude, service and performance are all interrelated.

In each case an effort was made to evaluate the fundamentals of the scheme, including:

- Offering the service
- Choice of language
- Customer-led practice
- Departmental schemes
- Monitoring the scheme
- The internal customer
- Translation requirement
- Staff appointments and training

In addition an evaluation was conducted on how the public consultation was organized, since this is a statutory requirement of the ratification process for the scheme.

In order to examine these elements detailed case studies of eight Welsh bodies were undertaken. The sample was comprised of five local authorities, namely Conwy, Gwynedd, Carmarthen, Caerphilly and Cardiff, and three public bodies, namely the North Wales Police, Carmarthen Health Board and Pembroke National Park Authority.

In addition the experience of Crown bodies and state departments in the UK was also investigated. Thus case-study material was derived from the following:

- The Home Office: ten departments
- The Central Office of Information
- The Department for Work and Pensions, including the DWP Network Agencies, e.g. Jobcentre Plus, Pension Service
- The Disability and Careers Service, the Child Support Agency and other businesses.

The main data sources for public bodies in Wales were in-depth interviews, the perusal of relevant files and reports, and participant observation. Interviews were held with language officers, senior managers, staff who were not directly responsible for the schemes, and politicians on a national and a local level. No interviews were held with customers as the remit of the investigation was to examine the internal workings of the schemes and their legislative context. The main information derived from UK government departments was data gathered at interviews together with the analysis of official documents, reports and deliberations within and between departments. Interviews were held with language officers and heads of department in the Home Office, the Central Information Office and the Department for Work and Pensions, and with other civil servants who were not directly responsible for the schemes. A comprehensive analysis was also conducted on data and material generated by Crown bodies and governmental departments.

Results: Public Organizations

Only selected key results are given here in order to inform the evaluation of the performance of the Language Act. However, even in summary form it is clear that there is strong evidence of compliance with the Welsh Language Scheme (WLS) guidelines. The introduction of WLS has transformed public administration in Wales by ensuring a new mindset with regard to operating bilingually. The language agenda is now part of the routine professional development of the public sector. However, the sector continues to face several challenges, notably in relation to the wide variation identified in the operation and implementation of language schemes. Such inconsistencies call into question the sufficiency of the current arrangements, under the Welsh Language Act, in guaranteeing minimum expectations of adequate service delivery and standards.

Gwynedd County Council represented the most constructive best practice found in the sample. The council operates internally through the medium of Welsh, all memoranda and internal communications are in Welsh, as is its correspondence with other public bodies in Wales. Gwynedd has adopted a proactive policy which goes far beyond the guidelines of the 1993 Welsh Language Act. In this respect Gwynedd is the closest we have to a successful model of bilingual operation.

It is evident that the ability of the majority of the population to speak Welsh is the main factor contributing to Gwynedd Council's commitment and capacity to function bilingually. Yet without committed political leadership exercised by the heads of organizations, it is unlikely that routine decisions will automatically favour Welsh as an official and *de facto* language in strongly Welsh-speaking areas. The density of Welsh-speakers does not necessarily lead to extensive use of the language within public bodies. Thus the determination shown by senior management has a strong influence on the commitment of the organization. This was very evident in the case of Gwynedd, Conwy and particularly the North Wales Police where the chief constable had been extremely supportive and proactive in increasing the practice of offering bilingual service to the public. By contrast where there a visible lack of leadership and commitment, it is unlikely that the WLS will fulfil the requirements of the organization and the public. Apathy and an insular attitude towards the Welsh language characterized those cases where there was no obvious commitment to the WLS on the part of political leaders or heads of departments. In turn this was often accompanied by a lack of close, regular consultation with the Welsh Language Board.

Bilingual services

Again Gwynedd led the way in the delivery of bilingual services as it is the norm for public-service behaviour there. Gwynedd readily engages in Welsh-medium written documentation, the discussion of complex matters in Welsh, together with effective correspondence and the creation of a positive and supportive bilingual work culture. It has been successful in developing its bilingual corporate identity in its relations with other public institutions. By contrast, most of the other organizations in the sample provided an incomplete service, although there are signs of a gradual improvement. Much has been done to raise language awareness within some sectors such as the social-care and child-care sectors. Until very recently the vast majority of front-line staff in Welsh public institutions served the public in English only. But the requirements of the WLS guidelines together with pressure and advice from the WLB has resulted in the appointment of language officers and the delivery of Welsh language-awareness training courses (Welsh Language Board, 2006, 2008). The board justifies such investment in language training by arguing that it contributes to the improvement in the standard of public service delivery. Consequently as one of the six designated performance indicators, public authorities are required to record their success in evaluating the number of staff who have received language-awareness training and higher level Welsh skills training.

Training

Language training and awareness were particularly good in Gwynedd and North Wales Police, reasonable in other cases and weak in one other. Most local authorities had been content to appoint staff in the expectation that they would make an effort to learn or improve their Welsh. However all county councils and North Wales Police now take language skills into consideration when appointing. Naturally this strengthens their capacity to operate bilingually. Apart from statutory expectations and the board's professional support, it is clear that the special role of Rhwydiaith, private consultancy agencies and lobbying bodies has had a direct impact on service quality. Rhwydiaith's remit is to provide language officers with the opportunity to share their experiences and to provide training, especially on fulfilling WLS requirements. There are a number of specialist instructors who are active in the field and who have devised courses and materials to respond to employers' requirements and needs. The better training companies engage in a range of courses starting with language-awareness training, which presents basic statutory information about Welsh; moving on to bilingual development training, which deals with administrative procedures, before focusing on language-practice training, which deals with practical procedures and work practices together with the interrelationships of individuals in the workplace and the promotion of language sensitivity and appropriateness. What was not anticipated was the low number of official complaints received by councils and organizations from the general public. Consequently such citizen pressure did not weigh as heavily as the professional commitment of staff as an incentive to improve services. This needs further investigation, for in theory one would have expected a far higher degree of customer complaints operating as a driving force in the improvement of service delivery.

Resources

Resources and partnerships have an enormous impact on service quality. Face-to-face oral services tend not to be provided to the extent that would be expected in many situations. Welsh speakers have had to make special arrangements to use Welsh, and on a number of occasions evidence was obtained that the required material or service was available to the public in English only. Clearly then not all the measures contained in a WLS are implemented and there are examples of Welsh-language services suffering because of a lack of staff, lack of finance and lack of commitment. As a result one does not necessarily receive a high-quality service. In general county councils ensure a commitment to their language schemes when they lead partnerships and contract third-party operators. But in the case of other organizations there is strong evidence to show that when this is not the case there is a corresponding increase in the number of complaints regarding poor-quality service. Often unsatisfactory responses are received by complainants, some of which are forwarded to the WLB. Consequently there remain operational weaknesses in third-party services, in partnerships and increasingly, as the language is mainstreamed, in the core services of these institutions.

Implementation strategies

In respect of implementation strategies there are a number of particularly good examples, especially North Wales Police. Language officers are crucial to the implementation stage, and as a group they have matured to become a competent cohort of professionals, often working in difficult circumstances. As in every institution, on occasion, a clash can arise, between the specific requirements, the demands of the post and the interests of promoting Welsh throughout the organization. The evidence suggests that language officers are first and foremost answerable to their employers, and are acutely aware of their position within the larger organization. In general the language officers were relatively young, often in their first posts, full of enthusiasm for the language but learning how to operate within a very large organization. The most successful felt that they received support at the highest level, whether from a senior manager, a chief officer or chair of an institution. Those who were struggling felt that they were perceived mainly as translators and not regarded as facilitators with a strategic contribution to make to the institution. The evidence indicates that language-scheme objectives are sometimes hindered by a number of factors which are common across many institutions. They would include the reticence shown by middle management, a lack of practice/confidence among staff to operate bilingually and a lack of mainstreaming strategies by which Welsh could be given greater visibility and purchase in delivering services.

Processes

All of the organizations evaluated conduct regular internal audits on the nature of their services in order to identify weaknesses and poor practice. Yet to what extent these weaknesses were shared within the institution and with the Welsh Language Board is a different matter. For some the monitoring process itself was the crucial task; for others the aim was to try to ensure progress and the strengthening of the service. Although there were not many official complaints, the process of monitoring complaints tended to inform improvements in almost every case. Certainly the entire process benefits incrementally from the development of good practice as the schemes become approved for the second or third time. Thus sound practical ideas become mainstreamed throughout the system as the board reports back directly to the institution and routinely includes examples of good practice (anonymously) in the generic advice and guidelines offered to public bodies.

Acting on complaints

Over 3,100 complaints have been received since the board was established. The board's procedures for responding to and following up complaints are particularly good. The framework for recording, filing, responding to and investigating complaints is extremely balanced and professional. There is strong evidence that the board is conscientious in its monitoring and involvement with public bodies in Wales, chiefly because it wishes to work with them in a constructive manner rather than being viewed as a threat or as a body which polices language interests. Internal changes in the way the board's compliance officers have dealt with public bodies in the recent period have also led to closer cooperation so that organizations have increasing confidence in the board. But the board is much less effective in its dealings with Crown bodies and other organizations which disregard its injunctions and advice. In just a few serious cases the board has considered asking the minister to intervene. In truth the board is reliant more on persuasion and good practice than it is on statutory intervention and penalization. The board does not have the direct powers which some people assume are in its mandate. Unlike the situation in Ireland, the board cannot fine bodies or compensate those individuals from its own coffers who demonstrably have not received a reasonable standard of Welsh-medium services.

UK Government Departments

The number and scope of bilingual Welsh/English services available within the UK is much greater than was expected. The current research project investigated the impact of the Welsh Language Act on the work of the following UK government agencies: ten departments in the Home Office, the Central Office of Information, the Department for Work and Pensions, including the AGP Network Agencies, for instance Jobcentre Plus, Pension Service and Disability and Careers Service, the Child Support Agency and other businesses. While the headquarters of a number of government departments are located in London, Sheffield or Newcastle, several also have offices in Wales, with a prominent cluster located in Llanishen, Cardiff.

In contrast to the Gaelic Language (Scotland) Act 2005 which received Royal Assent on 1 June 2005 and was implemented on 13 February 2006, and deals with language matters within Scotland only, the scope of the 1993 Welsh Language Act, as part of Westminster legislation, extends to the whole of the British Isles, wherever services are offered to Welsh speakers. In consequence several agencies outside Wales offer a bilingual service. For example, the Student Loan Agency which offers finance to students throughout the UK is based in Glasgow and the government department which monitors animal movement is based in Whitehaven. Both are required to provide Welsh-medium services, employ Welsh speakers and are obliged to prepare a WLS.

In a number of cases the task of implementing the WLS has been devolved to unit managers, who in turn have recruited language officers. This was particularly the case of the Home Office as it dealt with the requirements of the Prison Service and the Police, and in the Department for Work and Pensions. Only a minority of such language officers were Welsh speakers, or even Welsh. Notwithstanding this, language officers and managers tend to be very committed to the language schemes. They recognized that it was a statutory requirement to implement language schemes in accordance with their professional training and obligation. In the case of the Central Office of Information, Jobcentre Plus, the Pension Service and the Disability and Careers Service, Welsh speakers acted as language officers, some having been appointed specifically to oversee the activities of a department in the wake of the new responsibilities occasioned by the WLS.

The UK civil service is undergoing structural change as its time-honoured departmental operating systems are being replaced by a more uniform and generic method of working. In one respect this makes it easier for good practice to diffuse from one part of the civil service to another. Nevertheless, in the case of language schemes there was hardly any interdepartmental cooperation or generic discussion regarding their implementation. The administrative culture of very large departments is essentially inward-looking and self-contained. In consequence it is almost impossible to justify holding a joint seminar or a joint language-awareness course for a number of staff in the London area. As a result of this lack of cross-fertilization, a number of examples were found of language schemes which had not been implemented owing to the lack of suitable staff, or the absence of any staff who had received in-service training to respond to the Welsh Language Act's requirements and the WLS guidelines.

This was due in part to a lack of recognition of the relevance of bilingual issues in some departments. However, it also stemmed directly from a lack of guidance, or political/administrative decisions by some UK ministers who refused to acknowledge their duties with regard to language schemes. One prominent case was David Blunkett's reluctance to implement the WLS while he was home secretary. Within three weeks of Charles Clarke becoming minister he had ensured that there was a process in place to deal with the procedure for compliance with the board's guidelines.

Another tendency was for civil servants to argue that since the vast majority of the work involved translating documentation and forms, it would only be a matter of time before machine-readable translations enabled them to offer the highest possible service in a range of languages, including Welsh. They saw little to distinguish the Welsh-speaking client/customer from those who spoke Gujarati or Urdu. They favoured a generic IT solution to the needs of Welsh speakers rather than seeking to construct a bespoke customized service to fulfil the requirements of the WLS.

The Evaluation of Language Schemes

The Welsh Language Board has a vital role in directing this process in Wales and beyond. The relationship between the board and a number of public bodies is maturing and developing as they share experiences and ideas and learn to have confidence in one another. Indeed it is fair to say that many of the language officers of public bodies have a great deal of valuable experience in implementing and monitoring the WLS and tend to share that with the WLB's staff. Some officers and local authority leaders have criticized the board for not regulating the WLS process more rigorously, though this can be interpreted as an excuse by the weakest for not committing themselves to the full implementation of the Act. In the early days of the operation of the WLS from 1996 onwards the board's operative culture and leadership tended to be far more prescriptive, since it wanted to ensure that the new process was successful. By today, after a decade or more of constructive co-operation, the board believes that the strongest and more robust public bodies can be trusted to implement and refine their schemes with a minimum of direct interference, since they often go far beyond the system's core guidelines. Indeed forward-looking bodies such as North Wales Police continuously raise public expectations and increase the pressure on other parts of the system e.g. the Home Office and other Welsh police forces to raise their standards.

Secondly the flexibility of language schemes reflects the maturity of the process. Indeed it is possible to envisage that different kinds of statutory guidelines could be prepared for various bodies. However, there are fears that with this type of subsidiarity flexible action may lead to complacency or to the WLB losing its core remit in directing the operation of the Act. One way of avoiding this would be to set robust targets for the mid-term; another way would be by standardizing and rationalizing the system, so that Crown bodies, especially, come under the board's direct regulation. Either way, the quality and nature of the service now needs to be deepened and improved.

Is the Act Effective?

The existing system is particularly good in developing an organization's capacity to prepare language schemes. However, it does not place a duty upon organizations to provide information to the board as required as part of any statutory investigation under Section 17 of the Act into the lack of implementation of a language scheme. Organizations have taken advantage of this weakness and have refused to cooperate and provide the board with basic information. In consequence the board's statutory powers should be strengthened in this respect.

The influence of the 1993 Act with regard to Crown bodies, such as UK government departments (including the Assembly Government) and a number of their agencies, is another specific example of the weakness of the current legislation. The board's powers to require organizations to prepare language schemes and then to approve them, do not extend to Crown bodies. Similar weaknesses may be noted with regard to the board's power to review the content of schemes, and in the case of the government, the power to insist upon the implementation of schemes. Rather the Board must depend upon the good will of Crown bodies. The weakness of being too reliant on goodwill has been manifest in the fact that some Crown bodies have taken twice as long as other bodies to prepare language schemes. Having said that, other Crown bodies have also prepared their schemes within six months. On other occasions Crown bodies have refused to implement the content of their language schemes – and political intervention at the highest level has been necessary to remedy the situation. Thus the key variables are the attitude and resources of the respective organization. In the case of the Crown bodies in general it is the fundamental power to oblige them to act which is lacking, not the mechanism of preparing and agreeing a scheme

This is neither acceptable nor reasonable. Consistency and clarity are needed, and the same expectations and standards should be imposed on Crown bodies as on other public bodies. The Assembly government has already suggested, in the evidence it provided to the Richard Commission, that Crown bodies should be brought completely within the scope of the 1993 Act. It is important that the government attempts to remedy this unacceptable situation before considering the transfer of substantial powers to a new regulator.

Under Section 10 (4)–(6) of the 1993 Act, the Assembly is required to obtain Westminster's approval for any revisions to the board's statutory guidelines on the preparation of language schemes. In the wake of devolution, and bearing in mind that it is the National Assembly that leads on this policy, I believe that it would be appropriate and timely for the Assembly to exercise the power to approve any revision to the statutory guidelines on the preparation of language schemes.

The 1993 Act also established the principle that Welsh and English should be treated on the basis of equality, as far as appropriate under the circumstances and as is reasonably practicable. An obvious tension exists within the above clause and on a practical level, and the language scheme is the instrument by which this tension could be resolved. Nevertheless it is fair to say that bodies often use the clause concerning appropriateness and reasonableness in a capricious way, so as to avoid having to take responsibility and act in a manner which treats both languages on the basis of equality.

It is due time that the clause dealing with appropriateness and reasonableness was repealed. Such a step, together with establishing Welsh as an official language in Wales would give a substantial impetus to, and reinforce, the status of Welsh. It would also demonstrate the government's commitment to the promotion and preservation of the language. And yet ultimately the chief weakness of the current system is that it is institutional responsibilities rather than individual rights which animate the legislative context. Thus the main features of the Act as it stands are that it has established a statutory foundation for the improvement of bilingual services, but the reluctance of Crown bodies and some other agencies to comply is an evident weakness. This specific element could be strengthened within the existing system. The lack of individual rights is a completely different matter, as is the demand for new legislation. This is because in comparison with 1993 the public sector has been transformed and there has been a fundamental change in the market-led provision of some core services, such as the former public utilities of gas, water and electricity supply. A more recent telling factor is the devolution of further powers from Parliament to the Assembly, best illustrated by the announcement of the Welsh Language Measure, 4 March 2010.

While the current investigation was concerned with the nature of provision and the attitudes of staff who were responsible for providing bilingual services, a second, unrelated research project was concerned with the experience of individuals who sought to obtain Welsh-medium public services. Its findings are suggestive and complement the current analysis.

And What about Usage?

The results of a second research inquiry, commissioned by the board, show that Welsh is used extensively in the public sector, and that this use stems directly from the implementation of language schemes. The Centre for European Research, Wales was commissioned to develop pioneering methods of measuring the degree to which Welsh is offered to the citizens by a range of public, voluntary and private bodies. The researchers note that the project had two main aims, namely (a) establishing a methodology so that the use of language in a bilingual society can be monitored over time, and (b) measuring the application of the methodology in six areas: Cardigan, Amlwch, Bangor, Machynlleth, Ruthin and Ammanford. The essence of the methodology was to develop indicators for language use via the development of a framework which treated language as an implicit process. The authors aver that they are 'moving away from simple concepts of language domains and diglossia' in order to 'try to provide exact measures of the way specific institutions use one language or the other, or both' (Centre for European Research, Wales, 2007: 3). The methodology was inspired by the Ofercat Project in Catalonia, which was established to inform new policies on increasing the day-to-day use of Catalan. Three key factors, language competence, the willingness to use this competence and the opportunities to use it, were fundamental to the process. In each of the six Welsh locations the framework was used to discover what the normative language was, and a hidden observation method was also used to reinforce the true nature of the process of use and language choice. The researchers were also required to identify whether or not a Welsh service was available when they visited government departments, councils, hospitals, shops and businesses. A total of 799 bodies were inspected at 942 different addresses.

Within each location researchers were asked to note language indicators such as whether staff spoke Welsh to them, whether there was Welsh or bilingual signage, whether publicity material was bilingual. Were bilingual websites evident, did bodies answer the phone bilingually and were they subsequently able to continue the conversation in Welsh? The work focused on organizations, not on individuals, on the premise that an organization is chiefly responsible for the language used by its staff.

As one would expect, the normative language used to greet visitors was English. Fewer than half the respondents were willing or able to use Welsh when the visitor spoke Welsh. The highest rate of use was amongst central government and local government officials. There was more use of Welsh in greeting people on the telephone, which was higher for instance than in the case of face-to-face interviews, but the rate was less than 50 per cent, with more use among public-sector services than in the voluntary sector. All central-government signage and most local government signs were bilingual. The health sector and theatres provided bilingual signage, while most voluntary-sector signage was in English only. Most organizations with English-only signage were small local organizations.

The level of courtesy observed in response to the use of Welsh was high, especially in face-to-face contacts, compared with a phone greeting by the respondent. A comparison of the use of Welsh with the proportion of the working-age population in each community who claimed that they could speak Welsh in the 2001 Census, demonstrates that only two out of the six communities, namely Bangor and Ruthin, had a higher than expected usage. The use of Welsh on websites and documents was more substantial in the public sector than in the private sector. The use of Welsh by individuals in social situations and entertainment varied from 18 per cent in Bangor, to 40 per cent in Cardigan, and within groups from 20 per cent in Bangor to 27 per cent in Amlwch.

The conclusions of this very interesting report are:

> While the use of Welsh is more prevalent in the public than the private sector, the provision of a Welsh language service cannot be taken for granted. The evidence suggests that the use of both languages is often provided by respondents who have only a limited grasp of Welsh and the subsequent use of Welsh is not possible. This can be interpreted more as a willingness to accommodate the use of Welsh than to embrace its use. If language use is a feature of social practice as institutionalised behaviour, with social practice thereby being largely tacit in nature, then the task of language planning and legislation is to legitimise a shift in the normative order. It involves redressing language use as a feature of a social practice, of which the individual is not necessarily aware. The evidence in this Report suggests that while public sector language schemes have been implemented, the full provision of Welsh language services is not available. Furthermore, any attempts to promote the use of Welsh in the private sector have met with only limited success. (Centre for European Research, Wales, 2007: 5–6)

Implications

The original 'From Act to Action' study has proposed a number of recommendations for the Welsh Language Board's attention as the research material has been presented in public meetings. The main findings have also been discussed with several of the Welsh Language Board's unit directors. One significant finding is that consideration could be given to conducting a review of the Welsh-language-scheme implementation process, in line with recent Estyn or the Audit Commission's auditing processes. Clearly best-practice conventions of agreeing and monitoring the WLS could be diffused to most organizations. A number of those interviewed asked for the Board's enforcement powers to be strengthened, so that the pressure to comply was not overly dependent on the persuasive powers of the language officers and other conscientious regulators within the institution. In January 2008 the board's internal systems for investigating complaints were strengthened. Consequently the board's officers have less discretion than previously in the implementation of the statutory procedures. Following this change of emphasis, the board's aim in relation to Sections 17–20 of the Act is to ensure that its powers are used to their full potential. It follows therefore that there will be an increase in the number of Section 17 investigations that are conducted, and it is reasonable therefore to expect that there will be an increase in referrals to the Heritage Minister. But this system is also unclear in the minds of a number of officers in public agencies in Wales and the UK who asked in the study for more clarification on the exact role and powers of the Assembly government to ensure the effectiveness of language schemes and statutory compliance.

Action

The political and legislative context in which language policy and language schemes operate is constantly changing. Among a number of factors which can affect the linguistic landscape of Welsh, consideration must be given to the cumulative influence of the proposals to reform the National Assembly (Welsh Office, 2005), the establishment of an Equality and Human Rights Commission, the Single Equality Bill, the influence and implications of extending discrimination law to include language, the need to require Crown bodies to draw up language schemes, the board's intention to search for more powers to investigate cases of non-compliance, together with the consequence of future action which recognizes the official status of Welsh in the UK and Europe.

The chief influence would be the character of any new language act, whether in Westminster or currently mandated as part of the Assembly's legislative programme. The impact of the Legislative Competence Order for the Welsh Language, having taken some two years to pass through all the scrutiny committees at Westminster and Cardiff Bay, has now empowered the Assembly to implement a full Welsh-language policy in line with its new responsibilities. Few major changes to the existing process of preparing or replacing language schemes will be forthcoming until 2011. But very quickly after that, or perhaps sooner if there is a sea change following general or Assembly elections, a decision may be expected on the reformulation of the Welsh Language Board and a new definition of the relationship between the promotional and implementation aspect of the board's current responsibilities.

Certainly the process of developing Welsh as a statutory element of public policy has moved from promotion to regulation. This justifies the establishment of the office of a language commissioner who would both protect and extend individual citizen language rights (Williams, 2007b). The commissioner would be expected to act as a champion and as a regulator. Given Ireland's experience, the commissioner should not be expected to be a 'popular' public servant, but nevertheless a highly effective one in safeguarding any statutory language interests. While it is clear that Welsh has a unique role within the UK, the opportunity should not be lost to argue also for the needs of Welsh-speakers in the wider international comparative context.

Thus the next steps will be concerned with how exactly the Assembly government enacts the new legislation for the Welsh language, how it extends language standards to cover parts of the private sector, especially private utilities, how it mainstreams the language as part of the equality agenda, and how new ways of conducting public administration are devised in line with the deliberative democratic recommendations proposed in Williams (2007a and 2007b). Above all there is a need for a new vision and robust leadership which will lead to increased resources, more language awareness and real skills training and holistic innovation. The current reformulation of Iaith Pawb is a positive recognition of the need for such improvement (Llywodraeth Cynulliad Cymru, 2003). Sound practice already exists in many contexts and public bodies have much to learn from the innovative and progressive approach of the North Wales Police, and Ceredigion and Gwynedd Councils. These bodies are characterized by a robust definition of the meaning of operating a bilingual institution, the creation of a truly bilingual workplace, the appointment and training of confident Welsh-speakers and the appreciation of bilingualism as a professional skill commensurate with many other elements of a high standard public-service delivery.

Conclusion

The results of the investigation indicate that bilingual services have improved dramatically but that there has been a lack of consistency and quality which prevent the public from receiving an equitable service. Although the flexibility of the system of agreeing language schemes is to be welcomed the element of compliance needs to be strengthened in relation to extending the board's statutory remit. A firm legal foundation and an effective language planning strategy would strengthen this aspect of language policy so as to construct a more robust national context within which a greater emphasis could be placed on service delivery at the local level.

The question may be asked whether the relationship between the main protagonists is too close. Further, what is the role of the citizen in influencing policy trends, both on a national and local level and in identifying needs and complaints? The best supportive evidence would be to witness a significant increase in the use of the services currently available, let alone agitating for them to be extended to new contexts. But to do this there needs to be a change in the attitudes, behaviour and expectations of many actors and agencies within the system. This is not just a matter of improving staff language awareness in progressive, committed organizations. There are deep structural problems in our education system in that it does not ensure that our workers have the key requisite communicative skills as they enter the employment market. Of course this is true also of our behaviour as customers. Legislation can create new opportunities but it is the socialization processes, chiefly the education system in a strong civil society, which develops an ability and desire to make the most of the opportunities available.

Acknowledgements

This is a revised version of a paper delivered to the Welsh Language Board Research Conference, Cardiff, 26–7 September 2007. It represents my interpretation of the situation, and the board is not responsible for any statement or criticism offered here. The material on legislation in Finland, Ireland and Wales was prepared as part of the 'Legislation to Action' project under the direction of Siv Sandberg, Peadar Ó Flatharta and Colin H Williams. The work was commissioned by Foras Na Gaeilge, Svensk Kulturfonden and the Welsh Language Board. I wish to thank my colleagues Diarmait Mac Giolla Chriost, Steve Eaves and Ifor Gruffydd for their assistance with the case-study fieldwork. I also wish to thank Meirion Prys Jones for granting me access to Welsh Language Board data and to his colleagues in the board for assisting me to interpret their professional duties in the field.

Notes

[1] The title of the project is 'From Act to Action' and the research work was carried out between 2005 and 2007 as part of a team from Ireland, Finland and Wales. Since then, with funding from the British Academy, I have been expanding upon parts of the research work to examine the legislative situation and bilingual/multilingual services in Canada, USA, Catalonia and the Basque Country.

References

Centre for European Research, Wales (2007). *Language Use Indicators: Final Report*, Cardiff, Welsh Language Board.
Commissioner of Official Languages (2005). Annual Report 2004–5, Ottawa, Commissioner of Official Languages.
—— (2007). Annual Report 2006–7, Ottawa, Commissioner of Official Languages.
Cymdeithas yr Iaith Gymraeg (2005). *Deddf Iaith Newydd: Dyma'r Cyfle*, Aberystwyth, Cymdeithas yr Iaith Gymraeg.
HMSO (1993). *Welsh Language Act*, London, HMSO.
Llywodraeth Cynulliad Cymru (2003). *Iaith Pawb: A National Action Plan for a Bilingual Wales*, Cardiff, Welsh Assembly Government.
Welsh Office (2005). White Paper, *Gwell Trefn Lywodraethu Well i Gymru* by the Welsh Office, part of the United Kingdom government, 15 June 2005, Cardiff and London, Welsh Office.
Williams, C. H. (2005). *Deddfwriaeth Newydd a'r Gymraeg*, Welsh Language Board lecture: Eisteddfod Eryri, 4 August.
—— (2007a). 'Deddfwriaeth Newydd a'r Gymraeg', *Contemporary Wales*, 19, 217–93.
—— (2007b). *Linguistic Minorities in Democratic Context*, Basingstoke, Palgrave.
Welsh Language Board (2006). *Language Awareness Training*, Cardiff, Welsh Language Board (unpublished document).
—— (2008). *Language Awareness Training Pack*, Cardiff, Welsh Language Board.

Increasing Bilingualism in Bilingual Education

Colin Baker
School of Education
Bangor University

Introduction

Modern Welsh-medium education is often regarded as commencing in Ysgol Gymraeg Aberystwyth on 25 September 1939. The first HMI inspection of this school was conducted on 13 February 1948 (Welsh Department, Ministry of Education, 1948). The report states: '*Welsh is the language of instruction and the language of play ... This policy is rigidly adhered to*' (p. 3). However, the report also mentions that children learnt English folk songs, were taught arithmetic in the top class through English, and English was used for English language and literature lessons. Thus the first modern Welsh school used two languages for teaching and learning. There was a distribution of two languages that emphasized Welsh.

Some seventy years later, with a much-expanded system of bilingual education that is internationally renowned, Wales has much experience in the use of Welsh and English in the classroom. Yet the curriculum allocation of two languages appears little more reasoned or researched than in 1939.

Our teachers use two languages; we rarely train them for such use. Teachers allocate two languages for teaching and learning; we have almost no evidence across the nation about such distribution. Schools in Wales are ambiguously called bilingual and Welsh-medium (Welsh Assembly Government, 2006), yet neither a theoretically sound rationale nor an evidence-based bilingual teaching and learning methodology is available. Since 1939, there has been a growth in bilingual education but little growth in explaining overtly when, where, how and why two languages are used in the classroom. This is the substance of this paper.

To begin to unravel the issue of language allocation in a bilingual classroom, a simple question is: 'What is bilingual about bilingual education?' The answer is surprisingly complex. 'Bilingual education' is sometimes a label used for schools that contain bilingual children, but it is not their mission to produce bilingual and biliterate pupils. Other times, bilingual education is a term for schools where almost all, or all of the teaching is through an indigenous language. The children become bilingual through experiencing an indigenous language at school and a majority language out of school. In Wales we have some such schools in both Welsh heartland and predominantly English-language communities (Lewis, 2004).

This suggests that bilingual education is not always particularly bilingual. Three examples indicate that the term 'bilingual education' tends to hide within it approaches and strategies that are less than bilingual. *First*, there is a case of transitional bilingual education in the United States. From the 1960s to the turn of the century, one form of education particularly for recent immigrants was early-exit transitional bilingual education. In early-exit transitional bilingual education, a child whose home language is not English is allowed to use their home language in the classroom for one or two years (Baker, 2006). The main purpose of such education is fast transition from a heritage language to working in the curriculum only in English. In essence, this model contains bilingual children but does not aim to produce bilingual, biliterate or bicultural children. The aim is for cultural and social assimilation and not the retention of linguistic diversity or cultural pluralism. The label 'bilingual education' mostly refers to the children and not to education.

The *second* example is the case of designated bilingual schools particularly in predominantly English communities across Wales. In some of these designated bilingual schools, the curriculum is taught almost solely through the medium of Welsh (Williams, 2002), with the exception of English language and literature lessons. Not only will history and geography, physical education and information technology be taught through the medium of Welsh, but also science and mathematics. Given that such children often derive from English-language families and from predominantly English-language communities, keeping a balance between Welsh and English by Welsh-language schooling seems justifiable. The label 'bilingual education' tends not to refer to a curriculum delivered in two languages, or to strategies of teaching and learning that purposively use two languages.

The *third* example is that of dual language schools in the United States, or at least the '50:50' style of dual-language education (Lindholm-Leary, 2001). Since the mid-1960s, such schools have grown in number and status, and remained the most high-profile bilingual schools in the United States (Baker, 2006). Teaching through Spanish and English predominantly, but also through French and English, Chinese and English and Korean and English, the concept of language boundaries is part of the philosophy of this type of bilingual education. Both languages may be given equal weighting in the curriculum, and children become fluent and literate in both languages.

Proponents of the dual-language school movement have argued that the two languages should be kept separate in the classroom. In the United States dual-language model, using both languages simultaneously in a lesson is considered dangerous, as children will tend to use their stronger language, wait for the teacher to give instructions and explanations in their stronger language, resulting in one language, particularly English, being increasingly used to the exclusion of the other (Valdés, 2004). The aim is to produce bilingual children, and the use of both languages in the curriculum makes the dual-language model a 'strong form' of bilingual education (Baker, 2006).

Compartmentalization of the languages is achieved by teaching through one language one day, the other language on the next day. Or alternatively, one language is used in the morning, and the other in the afternoon, reversing this on the next day. This ensures that both languages are used in all curriculum areas. For example, Spanish is used to teach mathematics on Monday, Wednesday and Friday, with English the medium of instruction on Tuesday and Thursday. This is reversed in the following week. Another variation is to teach one whole week through one language, and the following week through a different language. In the 50:50 dual-language model, an equal balance is achieved in the use of each language in the curriculum. One essential objective is to maintain boundaries between the languages, avoiding code-switching by either teachers or students. However, in reality this does not stop children informally switching languages in private conversations and group work in the classroom.

Language Separation

The three examples are similar in that, in teaching and learning methodology, the aim is to separate languages, maintain boundaries and compartmentalize their use. In these three examples, both languages are typically not used in the same lesson. Bilingualism in the children is certainly an aim in the dual-language model. Nevertheless, this is achieved by monolingualism in a specific lesson period. Other forms of bilingual education tend to have a similar rationale. An example: in heritage language education the accent is placed on maximizing use of the heritage language within lesson periods. In Canadian immersion education, French and English are usually kept separate in the curriculum.

The principle of language compartmentalization in bilingual education appears to relate to (1) giving increasing time to the majority language when assimilation is predominant or (2) giving protected and sometimes maximal time to an indigenous or heritage language to optimize fluency, literacy, confidence and positive attitudes regarding that language, (3) avoiding inefficiencies in translation and duplication in the educative process (this will be discussed later) and (4) prejudices that still exist about bilinguals becoming mentally confused if two languages are active.

The principle of language separation is also based on avoiding code-switching among children. One concern in many minority-language situations is the development of an unstable code-switching among schoolchildren. The use of words such as 'Spanglish' (for a mixture of Spanish and English) and 'Wenglish' (for a mixture of Welsh and English) highlights a concern that mixing of languages can be a half-way house, indicating a movement away from a minority language towards the majority language. When children mix two languages, then there is a danger that this is a movement across time in those communities from bilingualism in Welsh and English towards English monolingualism. So language separation in school is often supported to strengthen and maintain the purity and integrity of a minority language such as Welsh.

The principle of language separation in bilingual education also relates to ideas from sociolinguistics, family language planning and language assessment in education. This is now discussed with the suggestion that language separation in the classroom links with wider views about: the functional separation of a minority and majority language to enable that minority language to survive (reserved functions); the one-parent – one-language method of raising children bilingually from birth; and the tendency in education (e.g. assessment) to value and legitimate the majority language at cost to the minority language.

Language separation in education relates to the concept of diglossia. Within the concept of diglossia is the notion that language communities tend not to use both languages for exactly the same purposes. While there are inevitable overlaps, one language tends to be used in certain situations, with certain people and for certain purposes, with the other language being used in different situations, with a different set of people and for different purposes. Fishman (1972, 1980) argued that when there is not compartmentalization of languages, as in the case of bilingualism without diglossia, and either language is used for almost any purpose, then the minority language tends to be unstable and downward language shift is highly likely. When there is not separation in usage of the two languages in the community, then Fishman (1980) argued that the minority language will decay in its status and usage, and the majority language will successively increase in its powerfulness, status and use. Therefore, language planners sometimes advocate reserving specific functions for the minority language, such as in particular cultural activities (e.g. Welsh-only use in eisteddfodau) and occasionally in niche economic activities (e.g. Gaeltacht in Ireland).

Since bilingual education, such as the dual-language model, seeks to use both languages, or at the least produce bilingual and biliterate children, then bilingual education in itself seems to work against functional separation. However, separation occurs by reserving different time periods, locations, curriculum subjects, even teachers for each language. For example, in some bilingual schools, the humanities subjects are taught through the minority language while maths and science are taught through a majority language such as English.

The doctrine of language separation in bilingual education relates to advice from experts on the raising of bilingual children in a family. In particular, for over a hundred years, the OPOL method has been consistently praised by academics and families (Barron-Hauwaert, 2004). OPOL stands for 'one parent – one language' simultaneous child language acquisition in the family. Each parent will speak their own language to the child from birth, so that the child hears two languages from two different people. For example, the mother may speak Welsh to the child, and the father speaks English. This method has been extolled in the literature as it creates language separation for a very young child (Piller, 2002). Rather than the child hearing a mixture of Welsh and English, there is a clear separation of the two languages with boundaries set by the parents. As such, it seems to produce an efficient dual-language input and highly fluent bilingual children. Language compartmentalization is advocated – and case studies suggest OPOL leads to much success (Baker, 2006). This tends to mirror the principle of dual-language schools in the United States with compartmentalization of the two languages, sometimes achieving separation by a different teacher who uses a different language.

Language separation is also evident in language assessment, for example when children have language disorders, delays or developmental problems. Typically, the educational or clinical psychologist assesses the child in the majority language of the country and not in the child's minority language. The norms that are used tend to be that of the monolingual, majority language speaker. When both languages are assessed, the benchmark tends to be monolinguals and not bilinguals.

Contrasting Views about Bilinguals

Cook (1992) and Grosjean (2001) suggest two divergent views of bilinguals: one about separation, the other about 'wholeness'. The fractional view of bilinguals sees the individual as two monolinguals in one person. For example, if English is the second language, scores on English tests will typically be compared against native monolingual Anglophone norms.

One consequence of the fractional view is to believe that 'proper bilinguals' are approximately equally fluent in both languages, with proficiency comparable to a monolingual. If competence does not exist in the majority language, then bilinguals may be maligned and classed as substandard. In the United States, for example, minority-language children in bilingual education are often classified as LEP (Limited English Proficient). The monolingual is seen as normal, and the bilingual as unusual or peculiar. Many bilinguals accept this stereotype, and a self-fulfilling prophecy makes them feel insufficiently competent in one or both of their languages compared with monolinguals, accepting and reinforcing the monolingual view of bilinguals. A bilingual may apologize to monolinguals for not speaking their language as well as they do.

Yet the bilingual is a complete linguistic entity, an integrated whole. Thus Grosjean (2001) offers a much more positive 'holistic view'. In athletics, could we fairly judge a sprinter or high jumper against a hurdler? The sprinter and high jumper concentrate on excellence in one event. The hurdler develops two different skills, trying to combine a high standard in both. The hurdler may be unable to sprint as fast as the sprinter or jump as high as the high jumper. This is not to say that the hurdler is an inferior athlete to the other two. Any such comparison makes little sense.

In Wales, a bilingual's English competence is measured by first-language English tests, and compared with the performance of monolinguals. In school examinations, in primary and secondary school, bilinguals in Wales are expected to perform as well in English as English-language monolinguals.

When someone learns English as a second language, should that competence in English be measured against monolinguals or other bilinguals? In countries such as the United States, for economic and political assimilation reasons, a politically dominant view is that bilinguals should face the same English assessments in school. In Australia, most of Canada, the United States and the UK (including Wales), dominant English-speaking politicians and administrators will not usually accept a different approach or standard of assessment (one for monolinguals, another for bilinguals). Language separation is thus reinforced as a principle in bilingual education by the dominance of the fractional viewpoint about bilinguals, and little or no understanding of what a holistic view of bilinguals might suggest in terms of classroom teaching and learning methodology.

The fractional and holistic viewpoints parallel ongoing research on the representation and storage of language in the bilingual brain. One issue has been whether a bilingual's two languages function independently or interdependently. A separate storage notion suggests that bilinguals have two independent language storage and retrieval systems with the only channel of communication being a translation process between the two separate systems. A shared storage idea indicates that the two languages are kept in a single memory store with two different language input channels and two different language output channels. Evidence suggests that lexical representations for each language are separately stored by a bilingual, but (and importantly for bilingual methodology in the classroom) conceptual representations are shared (Bialystok, 2001). For example, if a person has been taught the concept of gravity in one language, to understand it in another language does not require teaching it again in that second language. Rather, once a child has understood it in one language, it is understood per se, and can be spoken about in either language so long as the lexical resources are available. However, this does not exclude the teaching opportunity for a concept to be relayed in one language, and reinforced in another.

Studies also show that both languages remain active when just one of them is being used. For example, when someone is speaking in Welsh, in terms of brain activity English is also active and can be immediately accessed and instantaneously used by a bilingual speaker. In the functioning of the brain, one language does not lie dormant when the other is being used. This has implications for bilingual teaching methodology, and for the strategic use of both languages rather than for strict compartmentalization.

Language Allocation in Bilingual Classrooms

So far, this paper has considered the typical arrangement of two languages in a bilingual school. It has suggested that the principle of language separation, language boundaries and language compartmentalization has been dominant in pedagogical thinking. This has been linked with viewpoints from sociolinguistics, child rearing and viewpoints about bilinguals that each provide a wider context for such a language separation principle to have gained acceptance. It is rare for any bilingual education system in any country of the world to believe manifestly in the use of both languages in the same lesson. The accepted pedagogy has become to arrange the use of two languages to remain detached and discrete. This paper challenges that accepted pedagogy, and raises a question that it is difficult if not impossible to answer from current research, and that is: How do different language allocation strategies in a bilingual classroom relate to pupil achievement? Does separation of languages result in higher curriculum performance by children? Might strategic use of two languages result in higher attainment?

Before examining these issues in more detail, it is important to contextualize this discussion in the many schools and classrooms in

Wales that contain a mixture of Welsh-first-language and Welsh-learner children. In a mixed-language classroom where some children are totally fluent in Welsh and others are newcomers, a well defined policy and practice in language allocation is required (Lewis, 2004). Where children in linguistically mixed classrooms have different levels of ability in the two languages, as well as different levels of ability in tackling the curriculum, a dual-language methodology may be essential. In Wales, a class may contain children who are relative beginners in Welsh (e.g. recent immigrants), those with some second-language Welsh fluency and native Welsh speakers. A school that aims to achieve a high standard of ability in both languages will need to consider the use and allocation of languages in classrooms and across the curriculum.

The Construction of Language Separation

For proponents of the principle of language separation in a classroom, how should languages be separated in a classroom? There are basically eight non-independent dimensions along which the classroom separation of languages occur:

Subject or Topic

Different curriculum areas may be taught in Welsh and English. For example, humanities and physical education may be taught through Welsh with mathematics, science and computer studies taught through English. In pre-school and primary schools, the allocation may be by topic rather than subject. For example, a project on 'Dress' may be through the medium of Welsh, a project on 'Water' through the medium of English. Curriculum areas such as history and geography are often regarded as best taught through the heritage language. In contrast, science and technology may be seen as international, with its literature and research dominated by English. The jeopardy is that the Welsh language becomes associated with past culture and tradition, and the present with twenty-first century technology and science becoming identified with a view that science is white, Western and English-language. In contrast, one more neutral and effective practice in the United States found in dual-language education is for a teacher to write in blue for English and in red for Spanish.

Person

The use of two languages in a school may be separated according to person. Just as in the OPOL 'one parent, one language' system, so different school staff may be identified with different languages. For example, there may be two teachers working in a team teaching situation. One teacher communicates with the children through English, the other teacher through Welsh. Alternatively, teachers' assistants, parents helping in the classroom, auxiliaries and paraprofessionals may function in a different language from the teacher.

Time

A frequently used United States strategy in language allocation in schools is for classes to operate at different times in different languages, with variation by lessons, half-days, whole days, weeks or months. This may include a policy that varies by year group and age. For example, children may be taught in Welsh for the first two or three years of primary education for 100 per cent of time. Over years 3 to 7, an increasing amount of curriculum time may be allocated to the English language.

Place

Another process of classroom language separation is via different physical locations for different languages. In Canadian immersion schools, students occasionally have different classrooms for French and English lessons, paralleling the diglossic idea of functional separation. The assumption is that a physical context provides a sufficient reminder to use only one language in a particular place. In reality, the teacher and classmates may be more influential in signalling which language to use. A consideration of 'place' in language allocation needs to include all areas of the school. All areas in a school accumulate to create a language ethos and thus influence language choice by children.

Medium of activity

Another form of separation is between listening, speaking, reading and writing in the classroom. For example, the teacher may give an oral explanation of a concept in Welsh, with a follow-up discussion with the class also in Welsh. Then the teacher may ask the children to complete their written work in English. This sequence may be strategically reversed in a subsequent lesson. Another example would be children reading material through English, and then invited to write about it in Welsh. The aim of this teaching strategy is to reinforce and strengthen both learning and language among all children. By reprocessing the information in a different language, greater understanding may be achieved. However, this begins to merge with the concurrent use of both languages in a lesson – a strategy of using both languages in the learning process. This idea of a sequenced use of two languages in learning is considered later.

One risk of 'different medium' separation is that one language is used for speaking and another language for reading and writing. Where a minority language does not have a written script this may be a necessary boundary. Even when a minority language has written materials, the danger is that the minority language will be identified with oracy and the majority language with literacy with a potential effect of giving higher importance and more uses to the majority language and its associated literacy.

Curriculum material

There are a variety of ways in which written, audio-visual and information technology curriculum material can be delivered in two languages, ensuring separation and non-duplication. Course materials may only be allocated in one language with the oral teaching in another language. This is separation 'across' curriculum material; there is also separation possible 'within' such material as in dual-language books (e.g. with English on one side of the page and Arabic on the other, sharing the same pictures; see Edwards, 1995).

Function

In the United States schools and classes where there are bilingual children, there is sometimes teaching in the majority language while the management of the classroom occurs in the minority language. For example, in US schools with many Spanish speakers, the teacher may transmit the 'formal' subject matter in English, while conducting 'informal' episodes in Spanish.

Student

The previous seven dimensions have suggested that a school or a teacher may inaugurate a policy about dual-language use in a bilingual classroom. However, children themselves often define the language that is used in a classroom. To explain something clearly, the student may switch to his or her preferred language. Children may feel more at ease talking to teachers in their minority language in private conversations.

The Contemporaneous Use of Two Languages in a Lesson

The contemporaneous use of two languages in a bilingual classroom tends to be regular in practice, but rare as a predetermined teaching and learning strategy. Jacobson (1983, 1990) suggested that the integrated use of both languages rather than language separation can be educationally beneficial. Four contemporaneous uses are now considered.

Switching languages

In many bilingual classrooms, code-switching between two languages, particularly in small groups of children, is fairly typical. Code-switching is a term used to describe any switch within the course of a single conversation, whether at word or sentence level or at the level of blocks of speech. Baker (2006) suggests twelve overlapping purposes of code-switching such as substitution, emphasis, reinforcement, clarification, checking meaning, and signalling status and identity in a relationship.

Monolinguals may have negative attitudes to code-switching, believing that it shows a deficit, or a lack of mastery of both languages. However, it tends to be those who are more fluent in a language that code-switch (Meisel, 2004). Bilinguals have a choice of using both languages as a style of communication, and this is often achieved in a controlled, predictable and cognitively efficient manner (Moore, 2002; Jaffe, 2007; Van der Walt, 2006). Thus Lin (1996) has shown that the patterns of code-switching in Hong Kong classrooms are predictable and patterned. Such movement between two languages has both pedagogic and social functions (e.g. increased comprehension of meaning as well as decreasing personal distance). Code-switching by the teacher may signal the start of a lesson or a transition in the lesson, specify an interaction with a particular child or the move from teaching content to classroom management and discipline.

Van der Walt (2004) suggests that there is 'responsible codeswitching' that explicitly attempts to use the home language to make instruction more meaningful, making connections between two languages, and developing both languages simultaneously. In this sense, responsible, well-monitored, systematic code-switching uses alternation between two languages for pedagogic and linguistic development, and suggests that compartmentalization is both artificial and inefficient in increasing understanding among pupils, and in Van der Walt's (2006) research, also in higher education. However, a danger is that the teacher switches increasingly to the majority language, as may occur in transitional bilingual education.

Translating

In some bilingual classrooms, teachers will repeat what they have previously said in another language. For example, the teacher may explain a concept in Welsh, and then repeat the same explanation in English. Everything is said twice for the benefit of children who are dominant in different languages. This is a practice in the mixed-language classrooms in Wales that contain first-language, almost fluent second-language learners and early learners of Welsh. The danger is that the pupil knows that the same content will be given in their preferred language and waits for that to occur. Such duplication appears to result in less efficiency, and potentially lesser achievement in assessments.

Preview and review

One strategy in the contemporaneous use of languages in a classroom is to give the preview in one language and then a fuller review in the other language. For example, a topic is introduced in Welsh to provide an initial understanding. Then, the topic is considered in more depth in English. This may be reversed.

Purposeful concurrent usage

Rodolfo Jacobson (1990) suggested a purposeful concurrent use of two languages. Equal amounts of time are allocated to two languages, and teachers consciously and strategically move from one language to another. There are discrete language episodes with distinct goals for each language with a planned change from one language to another. Jacobson (1990) proposed this strategy to strengthen and develop both languages, and to reinforce taught concepts by children processing them in both languages. A use of both languages, he suggested, contributes to a deeper understanding of the topic being studied.

Translanguaging

Imagine that a teacher introduces a topic in English, making some remarks in Welsh. Group work is conducted in pupils' preferred language. The teacher interacts with the small groups and individual students in either Welsh or English. The students complete the worksheet in English. This type of situation is unlikely to develop students' literacy in Welsh. The languages have an unequal status and use. To allow students to make progress in both languages, there needs to be strategic classroom language planning.

Cen Williams (1994, 1996) advocates that there are strategies that develop both Welsh and English successfully and result in high achievement. In particular he found 'translanguaging' to work well in secondary schools and further education in Wales. In 'translanguaging', the input (reading or listening) tends to be in one language, and the output (speaking or writing) in the other language, and this can be systematically varied. For instance, a geography worksheet is in English. The teacher then initiates a discussion on the subject matter in Welsh, switching to English to highlight particular terminology. The students complete their written work in Welsh. In the next lesson, the roles of the languages may be reversed.

Translanguaging has three potential advantages. Firstly, it may promote a deeper and fuller understanding of the subject matter. If the pupils have understood it in two languages, they have really understood it. It is possible, in a monolingual teaching situation, for pupils to answer questions or write an essay about a subject without fully understanding it. Processing for meaning may not have occurred. Whole sentences or paragraphs can be copied or adapted out of a text book or from dictation by the teacher without real understanding. It is less easy to do this with 'translanguaging'. To read and discuss a topic in one language, and then to write about it in another language, means that the subject matter has to be processed and 'digested'. Secondly, 'translanguaging' may help pupils develop skills in their weaker language. 'Translanguaging' attempts to develop academic language skills in both languages. As Ofelia García (2006) argues, 'strict compartmentalization of languages needs to cede some instructional space for putting the two languages alongside each other for purposes of study and comparison in order to develop children's metalinguistic awareness of their own bilingualism and biliteracy' (p. 171).

Thirdly, the integration of fluent Welsh speakers and Welsh learners of various levels of fluency is helped by 'translanguaging'. If Welsh learners are integrated with first-language Welsh speakers, and if sensitive and strategic use is made of both languages in class, then Welsh learners can develop their second-language ability concurrently with content learning.

Conclusions

This paper has shown that bilingual teaching and learning varies from (1) teaching monolingually, or increasingly monolingually, in a minority language to achieve bilingualism in children as in Welsh-medium education, (2) teaching bilingually to achieve a movement from a minority language to a majority language as in the United States transitional mode, (3) teaching through both languages so as to achieve optimal bilingualism and biliteracy in pupils. Such variation immediately expresses that classroom practices can only be fully understood in relation to language politics, language status, language policy and language planning. A bilingual school is not an island; pedagogical decisions do not operate in isolation from language debates and decisions in the wider society.

In decisions in Wales about language compartmentalization and language allocation in a bilingual classroom, there are pedagogical issues that need consideration to create an effective dual-language policy in a school. The language aims of the school in terms of Welsh-language preservation and bilingual competence require explication. Where Welsh is to be preserved in the children, then separation may need to be planned. Welsh and English are not equal in power or status in the eyes of even young children, with a movement towards English increasing as the teenage years approach. Fishman's (1980) warning about reserved functions for minority languages is still relevant in the twenty-first-century 'cool bilingual' Wales.

Where teachers are more enthusiastic about developing bilingualism and biliteracy, then decisions are needed about the allocation of each language. Fewer language boundaries may be desired and more contemporaneous use may be chosen. There may be a deliberate loosening of boundaries to ensure the development of two languages.

Neither the surrounding politics nor pedagogic decisions are the sole bases for making strategic decisions about school and classroom language allocation. The nature of the pupils must also be taken into account. For example, there may be a developmental strategy reflecting the age and language development of the children (Romero and Parrino, 1994). If the children's language development is still at an early evolutionary stage, boundary setting may be more important. With older children, whose languages are relatively well developed, the contemporaneous use of two languages may be more efficacious. Thus a uniform policy with regard to boundaries and concurrent use may be less reasonable than a progressive policy that examines different uses across years and across the Key Stages. Early pre-school separation may be important, but later on, in secondary school, more contemporaneous use may enable conceptual clarity and depth of understanding, and possibly accelerate cognitive development.

The language balance of the class is often an important factor in a language-separation decision (Lewis, 2004; Hickey, 2001). If all the children speak a minority or majority language, there may be ease in determining a language allocation. However, classes may be mixed, with differing balances of majority- and minority-language children. Who dominates numerically, linguistically and psychologically in the classroom? When the balance is tilted against language-minority children, a clear separation with the curriculum balance towards the minority language may be desirable. Whether the children in a school are language-minority children in a subtractive or additive situation will also impact on language-allocation policies.

A school policy needs to take into account 'out of school exposure' to the Welsh language in particular. Sometimes, an equal amount of time is advocated for two languages in the school, with half the curriculum in one language, the other half in a different language. If the child is surrounded by the English language outside the school (e.g. street, screen and shop), then the balance may need to be much more towards the minority language in school.

A school policy regarding the separation and integration of languages may need a more micro-definition. The above discussion of language separation along different dimensions (e.g. curriculum area, location, time, input and output) indicates the choices not only in timetable and lesson arrangement but also in terms of language use by teachers and pupils (e.g. code-switching).

There are also decisions to be made at school level about using two languages to deliver the curriculum in a maximally efficient manner with pupil achievement high on the list of priorities. For example, the use of two languages in a manner that duplicates content needs to be avoided. Where the same subject matter is exactly repeated in a different language, some pupils will go 'off task'. Yet in a mixed-language classroom, where there is a mixture of first- and second-language pupils, for the sake of comprehension a teacher may need to repeat information or use more individualized learning and small-group work. This may allow some language boundaries to be established, with different children addressed (e.g. by teachers' aides) in their preferred language. The allocation of languages may need to ensure that learning is non-repetitive, non-parallel, incrementally sequenced.

There is also a pragmatic consideration. If teachers are expected to operate contemporaneous use of two languages in a classroom, it assumes considerable management abilities, self-monitoring and reflective awareness. Teachers have to react to the moment, to individual pupils, with many situations being unplanned and unpredictable. Pupils themselves considerably affect and determine dual-language strategies in a classroom, needing to communicate their conceptual understanding or misunderstanding in an immediate and efficient manner.

It is a sad conclusion that there is almost no research that examines whether or not the contemporaneous use of two languages in the classroom, as advocated by Jacobson (1990) in the United States and Williams (1997) in Wales, is effective and advantageous or otherwise. There are classroom studies that suggest positive outcomes, but these are a mixture of illustrative case studies and well-argued advocacy (e.g. articles on CLIL in the special issue of the *International Journal of Bilingual Education and Bilingualism*, 5, 2007).

Since the first modern Welsh school was established on 25 September 1939, there are almost seventy years of teacher experience in language allocation and distribution in Wales's classrooms. The recording and synopsis, exchange and dissemination, analysis and investigation of those seventy years of experience is one of the major current weaknesses of bilingual education in Wales.

If a teacher asks, 'Where is your evidence about what works, for whom, at what age, with what language profiles of children, and why?', we seem little better informed by evidence than were the Ministry of Education inspectors in Ysgol Gymraeg Aberystwyth on 13 February 1948. Answering those questions is the task ahead.

References

Baker, C. (2004). 'Biliteracy and transliteracy in Wales: language planning and the Welsh National Curriculum', in N. H. Hornberger (ed.), *Continua of Biliteracy: An Ecological Framework for Educational Policy, Research and Practice in Multilingual Settings*, Clevedon, Multilingual Matters.

—— (2006). *Foundations of Bilingual Education and Bilingualism* (fourth edn), Clevedon, Multilingual Matters.

Barron-Hauwaert, S. (2004). *Language Strategies for Bilingual Families: The One-Parent-One-Language Approach*, Clevedon, Multilingual Matters.

Bialystok, E. (2001). *Bilingualism in Development: Language, Literacy and Cognition*, Cambridge, Cambridge University Press.

Cook, V. J. (1992). 'Evidence for multicompetence', *Language Learning*, 42, 4, 557–91.

Edwards, V. (1995). *Reading in Multilingual Classrooms*, Reading, University of Reading.

Faltis, C. (1990). 'New directions in bilingual research design: the study of interactive decision making', in R. Jacobson and C. Faltis (eds.), *Language Distribution Issues in Bilingual Schooling*, Clevedon, Multilingual Matters.

Fishman, J. A. (1972). *The Sociology of Language*, Rowley, Mass., Newbury House.

—— (1980). 'Bilingualism and biculturalism as individual and as societal phenomena', *Journal of Multilingual and Multicultural Development* 1, 1, 3–15.

García, O. (2006). 'Lost in transculturation: the case of bilingual education in New York City', in M. Putz, J. A. Fishman and N.-V. Aertselaer (eds.), *Along Routes to Power: Explorations of Empowerment through Language*, Berlin, Mouton de Gruyter.

Grosjean, F. (2001). 'Bilingualism, individual', in R. Mesthrie (ed.), *Concise Encyclopedia of Sociolinguistics*, Oxford, Elsevier Science.

Hickey, T. (2001). 'Mixing beginners and native speakers in minority language immersion: who is immersing whom?, *Canadian Modern Language Review*, 57, 3, 443–74.

Jacobson, R. (1983). 'Can two languages be acquired concurrently? Recent developments in bilingual methodology', in H. B. Altman and M.McClure (eds.), *Dimension: Language 1982*, pp. 110–31. Louisville, Ky., University of Louisville Press.

—— (1990). 'Allocating two languages as a key feature of a bilingual methodology', in R. Jacobson and C. Faltis (eds.), *Language Distribution Issues in Bilingual Schooling*. Clevedon, Multilingual Matters.

Jaffe, A. (2007). 'Codeswitching and stance: issues in interpretation', *Journal of Language, Identity, and Education*, 6, 1, 53–77.

Lewis, W. G. (2004). 'Addysg gynradd Gymraeg: trochi a chyfoethogi disgyblion', *Welsh Journal of Education*, 12, 2, 49–64.

Lin, A. M. (1996). 'Bilingualism or linguistic segragation? Symbolic domination, resistance and code switching in Hong Kong schools', *Linguistics & Education*, 8, 1, 49–84.

Lindholm-Leary, K. J. (2001). *Dual Language Education*, Clevedon, Multilingual Matters.

Meisel, J. M. (2004). 'The bilingual child', in T. K. Bhatia and W. C. Ritchie (eds), *The Handbook of Bilingualism*, Malden, Blackwell.

Milk, R. D. (1990). 'Integrating language and content: implications for language distribution in bilingual classrooms', in R. Jacobson and C. Faltis (eds.), *Language Distribution Issues in Bilingual Schooling*, Clevedon, Multilingual Matters.

Ministry of Education (Welsh Department) (1948). *Report by H.M. Inspectors on Yr Ysgol Gymraeg Aberystwyth, Cardiganshire*, London, Ministry of Education.

Moore, D. (2002). 'Code-switching and learning in the classroom', *International Journal of Bilingual Education and Bilingualism*, 5, 5, 279–93.

Piller, I. (2002). *Bilingual Couples Talk: The Discursive Construction of Hybridity*, Amsterdam, John Benjamins.

Romero, M. and Parrino, A.(1994). 'Planned alternation of languages (PAL): language use and distribution in bilingual classrooms', *Journal of Educational Issues of Language Minority Students*, 13, 137–61.

Valdés, G. (2004). 'Between support and marginalisation: the development of academic language in linguistic minority children', *International Journal of Bilingual Education and Bilingualism*, 7, 2 and 3, 102–32.

Van der Walt, C. (2004). 'The challenge of multilingualism: in response to the language policy for higher education', *South African Journal of Higher Education*, 18, 1, 140–52.

—— (2006). 'University students' attitudes towards and experiences of bilingual classrooms', *Current Issues in Language Planning*, 7, 2 and 3, 359–76.

Welsh Assembly Government (2006). *Defining Schools according to Welsh Medium Provision*, Cardiff, Department for Training and Education, Welsh Assembly Government.

Williams, C. (1994). 'Arfarniad o ddulliau dysgu ac addysgu yng nghyddestun addysg uwchradd ddwyieithog', unpublished Ph.D. thesis, University of Wales, Bangor.

—— (1997). *Bilingual Teaching in Further Education: Taking Stock*, Bangor, Canolfan Bedwyr, University of Wales, Bangor.

—— (1999). *Dulliau Dysgu ac Addysgu mewn Addysg Bellach*, Bangor, Canolfan Bedwyr, University of Wales, Bangor.

Williams, Cen, Lewis, G. and Baker, C. (1996). *The Language Policy: Taking Stock: Interpreting and Appraising Gwynedd's Language Policy in Education*, Llangefni, CAI.

Williams, I. W. (2002). *Gorau Arf: Hanes Sefydlu Ysgolion Cymraeg 1939–2000*, Talybont, Ceredigion: Y Lolfa.

Young People and their Use of the Welsh Language

Delyth Morris
School of Social Sciences
Bangor University

Introduction

Consecutive Censuses of Population have shown a steady increase in the percentage of young people who can speak Welsh in Wales. This increase has been generally welcomed, and the Welsh Assembly government, recognizing the potential of this pool of young bilingual speakers for the survival of Welsh, has made young people a specific target in its Welsh language strategy, *Iaith Pawb* (National Action Plan for a Bilingual Wales). It states:

> The Assembly Government is acutely aware that if Welsh is to flourish, young people in particular need to develop a sense of ownership for the language and to see it as their language and not simply the language of school and culture (2003: 4.38)

The Welsh Language Board, a statutory body established by the UK government as part of the Welsh Language Act 1993, and whose duty is to 'promote and facilitate' the use of the Welsh language, is entrusted with the duty of ensuring that this potential is utilized to the maximum advantage. While welcoming the encouraging upturn in the number and percentage of young Welsh speakers, the board however acknowledges that there is cause for concern that young people's knowledge of Welsh does not necessarily translate into language use. As a part of its remit to increase the social use of Welsh among young people, the Welsh Language Board commissioned a

Young People and their Use of the Welsh Language

report into young people's social networks and their use of language in those networks.[1]

Over the past century, the Welsh language has been in decline both numerically and in percentage terms. In 1901, approximately a million people, 50 per cent of the population of Wales, spoke Welsh, but by 2001 this figure was reduced to just 21 per cent of the population, around half a million in number. However, the 2001 Census also showed a significant increase in the incidence of Welsh speakers in the younger age groups, especially those aged between five and nine years, and also the 10–14 years and 15–19 age groups.

This increase in the percentage of Welsh-speaking young people was first noted in 1981, and the results of the 1991 and 2001 Censuses confirmed the general upward trend. The dramatic increase experienced in 2001 has been attributed partly to the increased role of Welsh in the National Curriculum, where it is a core subject studied by all children in Wales between 7 and 16 years of age in Welsh-medium education and a foundation subject for pupils in other schools in Wales. Welsh is also used as the main teaching medium in 448 primary schools in Wales, and 54 secondary schools are defined as

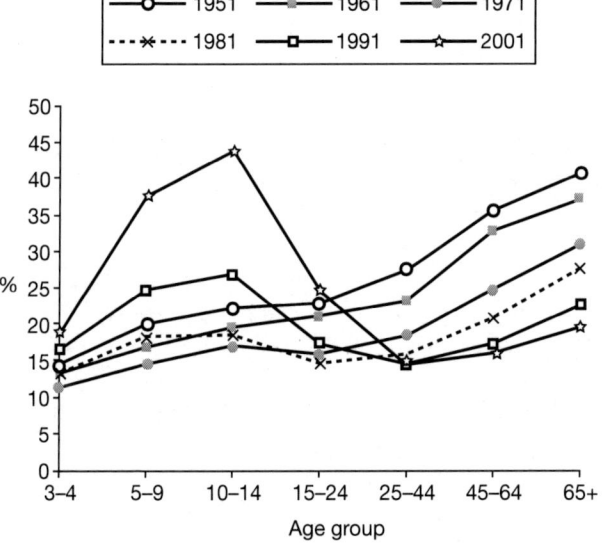

Diagram 1 Welsh speakers: percentage by age group 1951–2001 Census[2]
Source: Censuses of Population

Welsh Language Secondary Schools, where more than half the basic subjects are taught partially or entirely through the medium of Welsh. The demand for Welsh-medium education continues, especially in the more Anglicized areas of south Wales, such as Rhondda, Cynon and Rhymni Valleys and in Cardiff, where the community use of Welsh is relatively low.

The result of the increase in Welsh-medium education is that there are by now some 86,000 10–14-year-olds and 57,000 15–19-year-olds in Wales who can speak Welsh. However, the number of these young people who use Welsh outside the formal school environment is unknown.

The Study

The social network analysis study undertaken for the Welsh Language Board involved looking at the social networks and language use of twenty-four young people aged between 13 and 17 years in each of the 12 study areas across Wales between 2003 and 2005. A total of 9,000 interactions were studied in each area, making a total of over 100,000 interactions in all. By linking together the two factors – social networks and language use – it was possible to consider the relationship between them. The social contexts of language use considered were the home and family, friends and contemporaries, the community and social clubs and organizations.

Some of the localities chosen for the social networks study were areas where the Welsh Language Board has a Language Action Plan officer, whose aim is to encourage more use of Welsh within local communities through activities such as fun days for children, sports activities, and Welsh-language entertainment for young people. However, Aberystwyth, Bala, Lampeter and Ystradgynlais were not designated Language Action areas at the time of the study.

Aberystwyth is a seaside university town in mid-Wales, with a population of just over 11,000. It is estimated that around 50 per cent of the local population are Welsh speakers. The town also contains a large student population of approximately 7,000, with 5,000 of these coming from outside Wales. The town has two secondary schools, one designated bilingual and the other designated English-medium.

Amlwch is a harbour and post-industrial town in the north of Anglesey, in north west Wales. Tourism is important, as well as agriculture, and there is a large nuclear power station a few miles away. It has a population of 2,500, and 63 per cent of the population are Welsh-speaking. In recent years, there has been much in-migration to this area, partly connected to the nuclear power plant. The town has a bilingual secondary school.

Ammanford is a small town of 2,500 people located in a post-industrial valley in Carmarthenshire in west Wales, where 63 per cent of the population speak Welsh. The local secondary school is a traditional bilingual school.

Bala is a rural town in north Wales and is the focus for the large agricultural hinterland. The area is strongly associated with traditional Welsh culture. The population of the town is almost 2,000, and 81 per cent speak Welsh. The local secondary school, which has a huge catchment area, is bilingual.

Fishguard is a harbour town on the north coast of Pembrokeshire in west Wales, with ferry links to Ireland and a strong element of tourism in the local economy. The population is just over 3,000, and 40 per cent speak Welsh. The local secondary school teaches mainly through the medium of English.

Lampeter is a small market and university town in south-west Wales, with a population of 2,800, 52 per cent of whom speak Welsh. The student population is fairly small at 1,400. The local secondary school is designated bilingual.

Llandysul and Cardigan are two small towns situated twenty miles apart in south west Wales. Llandysul has a population of 1,500 with 71 per cent Welsh speakers. The local secondary school is a designated bilingual school. Cardigan is a market town with a population of 4,000 of whom 60 per cent speak Welsh. Although the local secondary school is designated as a 'traditional' bilingual school, the children of the area who wish to receive a bilingual education travel to the secondary school in Llandysul.

Llangefni is a market town in Anglesey in north-west Wales, and is the administrative centre of the island. The population of the town is almost 4,500, and 85 per cent are Welsh speakers. The local secondary school is a bilingual school.

Llanrwst is another market town, located in the Conwy Valley in north Wales. The hinterland is agricultural, and the tourist industry is prominent in the local economy. Llanrwst has a population of almost 3,000, and 65 per cent speak Welsh. The local secondary school is bilingual.

Machynlleth is a historic market town in mid-Wales with a population of just over 2,000, 55 per cent of whom speak Welsh, and the town is the shopping and administrative centre for the large rural hinterland. The local secondary school is a traditional bilingual school.

Pwllheli is situated in the north-west of Wales and is a small harbour town with a large marina. Tourism is a mainstay of the local economy. The town has a population of 3,700, and 81 per cent speak Welsh. The town is the centre for the large rural and agricultural hinterland of the Llyn Peninsula. The local secondary school is bilingual and there is also a Sixth Form College in the town for post-16 students.

Ystradgynlais is in south Powys near the county border with the industrial area of Neath Port Talbot. The population is almost 2,500, and 48 per cent speak Welsh. The local secondary school is designated English-medium, and pupils who wish to follow a Welsh-medium education travel to Ysgol Ystalyfera, two miles away.

Within each of these locations, a sample of twenty-four young people aged 13–17 years was selected to reflect their Welsh-language ability, together with the Welsh-language ability of their parents. The parental categories included three groups: both parents Welsh-speaking, one parent Welsh-speaking and the other non-Welsh speaking, and two non-Welsh speaking parents. Using these parameters, lists of potential respondents were drawn up and participants chosen on a random basis.

In all locations, the participation of the local secondary school was requested, and indeed their assistance was essential in choosing the respondents. Furthermore, their premises were used to undertake the interviews. Exceptions to this pattern involved the older respondents who had left school either to work or to undertake their post-16 education in other institutions. These were recruited independently, but with the assistance of the schools, who provided lists from among their previous pupils. The total sample size was 288.

The interviews were undertaken over a two-week period by interviewers who were drawn from the relevant location so that they would have knowledge of the area, its institutions and even some of the relevant networks. The interviewee was given the choice of completing the interview in either Welsh or English. In almost all cases, the interviews were undertaken on a sequential basis during a week of intensive work in each location. At the end of each interview, the respondents were asked to complete a diary of their activities during the subsequent week. These were returned and scrutinized by the interviewer during a second intensive week of work in each location.

The Results

Of the 288 respondents, 76 per cent had been born and raised in their present locality, while 11 per cent had moved from another part of Wales and 14 per cent had moved in from outside Wales. Just 13 per cent of the latter group were recent in-migrants, with most having lived in their present locality for between six and seventeen years.

Approximately two-thirds of the respondents' parents, 59 per cent of fathers and 62 per cent of mothers, were fluent or good Welsh speakers. However, only 35 per cent of the young people said that they spoke Welsh at home, with 43 per cent reporting that they spoke English only, and 22 per cent using both languages. Only 18 per cent of fathers and 15 per cent of mothers had no knowledge at all of Welsh.

Over half the respondents, 53 per cent, claimed to be fluent Welsh speakers, while 24 per cent noted they were fairly fluent and 23 per cent understood Welsh to varying degrees. Their confidence in using Welsh, however, varied, especially in different social situations.

Table 1 Confidence in the Use of Welsh with different interlocutors (%)

Context of use	Degree of confidence:					Total
	Very confident	Confident	Neutral	Not very confident	Not at all confident	
With adults you know	56	26	11	5	2	100
With close friends	55	29	7	7	2	100
With teachers	44	33	17	4	2	100
In a bilingual group	39	38	14	7	2	100
With contemporaries you do not know	27	27	24	16	6	100
With adults you do not know	26	26	21	21	6	100

(n=288)

The respondents felt most confident with people they knew well, but this decreased substantially with people they did not know. Not unexpectedly, the confidence of the sample was linked to their ability in the language, and although all had a knowledge of Welsh, and 77 per cent were able to speak Welsh, some still felt less than confident in their Welsh-language skills when speaking to adults and other young people they did not know. So while 99 per cent of fluent Welsh speakers were confident or very confident when speaking Welsh to close friends, this decreased to 76 per cent with young people they did not know well. It is apparent that communication involves more than learning a language fluently.

Most of the young people in the sample (96 per cent) had received their primary education in their present locality, with 57 per cent stating that Welsh was the medium of instruction, while 37 per cent had received bilingual instruction in both Welsh and English. Only 6 per cent had been educated through the medium of English. However, there was considerable variation between the localities on this point.

Table 2 Respondents who received their primary education through the medium of Welsh (%)

Locality	Welsh medium	Bilingual Welsh and English	English medium	Total
Pwllheli	92	4	4	100
Bala	88	13	0	100
Llangefni	67	29	4	100
Amlwch	63	29	8	100
Ystradgynlais	58	38	4	100
Aberystwyth	54	46	0	100
Ammanford	50	46	4	100
Llanrwst	50	46	4	100
Machynlleth	46	33	21	100
Lampeter	46	46	8	100
Fishguard	42	54	4	100
Llandysul/Cardigan	33	63	4	100

(n=288)

Looking more closely at the language of the respondents' interaction at primary school level, 76 per cent stated that they spoke Welsh only with their teachers, 12 per cent used both languages and 12 per cent spoke English only. The children also had considerable opportunity for discussion in class among themselves; however, just 46 per cent said that they spoke Welsh with other children in the class, while 33 per cent stated that their interaction was exclusively English. The others used a mixture of both Welsh and English during classroom interactions. During school breaks and outside the school, the percentage speaking exclusively English with other children rose considerably – to 49 per cent during school breaks, and 45 per cent outside the school.

In secondary school, the use made by respondents of Welsh reduced in every setting.

Table 3 Respondents' Welsh-language use in different settings at primary and secondary school (%)

	Primary	Secondary
Welsh-language use with teacher	76	51
Welsh-language use with other children in the classroom	46	30
Welsh-language use with other children outside the classroom	32	20
Welsh-language use with other children outside school	33	27

Table 4 Respondents' language of communication with interlocutors at primary school (%)

Locality:	Welsh-language use with teacher	Welsh-language use with friends in the classroom	Welsh-language use with friends during school breaks	Welsh-language use with friends outside school
Bala	100	79	79	75
Pwllheli	88	63	63	63
Aberystwyth	83	46	38	33
Fishguard	83	25	8	13
Llandysul/Cardigan	79	33	13	25
Ystradgynlais	75	46	8	8
Llangefni	71	67	50	54
Amlwch	71	38	29	25
Lampeter	71	38	33	29
Ammanford	71	29	13	17
Machynlleth	67	54	17	21
Llanrwst	58	38	33	29

(n=288)

In the case of table 3, although there was considerable variation in practice between the different localities, generally the pattern was of a relatively high use of Welsh with teachers compared with a relatively low use with friends, as table 4 shows.

Bala and Pwllheli had the highest rates of Welsh-language use with all the sets of interlocutors; by contrast, there was a sharp difference between the children's use with the teacher in the classroom and with friends outside the formal education setting, especially in Llandysul/Cardigan, Fishguard, Ammanford and Ystradgynlais. It appears that in many areas the primary school is not normalizing Welsh-language use among young children.

Table 5 Respondents' language of communication with interlocutors at secondary school (%)

Locality: language	Welsh-language use with teacher	Welsh-language use with friends in the classroom	Welsh-language use with friends during school breaks	Welsh-language use with friends outside school
Pwllheli	88	38	38	42
Bala	88	71	54	63
Aberystwyth	83	58	25	33
Llandysul/Cardigan	75	38	33	33
Ystradgynlais	63	17	0	4
Llangefni	58	33	29	54
Lampeter	58	25	17	21
Amlwch	42	17	4	17
Llanrwst	29	33	25	29
Machynlleth	17	33	17	21
Ammanford	17	0	0	4
Fishguard	0	0	0	4

(n=288)

Although most respondents in Bala and Pwllheli stated that they spoke Welsh with their teachers at secondary school, there was a marked decrease in the use of Welsh among respondents in Pwllheli both within the classroom, and with friends inside and outside the school. The decrease in Bala was smaller, but nonetheless evident.

The sharpest decrease in Welsh-language use with teachers between primary and secondary levels was seen in Machynlleth, from 67 per cent to 17 per cent, although 58 per cent of the young people in Machynlleth reported that they spoke a mixture of both Welsh and

English with their teachers at secondary school. A marked decrease in the use of Welsh with teachers was also apparent in Llanrwst, from 58 per cent to 29 per cent, and here again the respondents reported more of a tendency to use both Welsh and English with their teachers at secondary level. These tendencies appear to reflect the introduction of language streams at the secondary school level.

In all the localities, a substantial decrease was reported in the use of Welsh with friends and peers both inside and outside school. In Fishguard, Ammanford and Ystradgynlais, there were very low incidences of Welsh-language use among young people of secondary school age, even though 84 per cent of the respondents in each of the three areas were either very fluent or quite fluent Welsh speakers.

The Networks

The young people's networks were analysed according to their peer group, families, communities and social clubs. The network configurations across the various locations portrayed quite different responses in the use of Welsh, with the major determinant of the Welsh language density in the various networks being the language used by the respondent at home.

Peer Networks

Most respondents saw their friends daily or every other day. Thirty nine per cent said they spoke Welsh only or mostly with them, while 61 per cent spoke only or mostly English within their circle of five closest friends. Not unexpectedly, there was a greater tendency to use English within a mixed language-ability group.

It appears that the predominant influence on the use of Welsh within networks of friends was the language of the home.

Eighty-one per cent of the young people from Welsh-speaking homes had mainly or only Welsh-speaking friends, while 92 per cent of young people from English-speaking homes had mainly or only English-speaking friends. The respondents who came from bilingual backgrounds also tended towards the use of English with friends, with 67 per cent having mainly or only English-speaking networks of friends.

Table 6 Use of Welsh in peer networks by home language (%)

Home language:	Language of peer network:		Total
	Only or mainly Welsh	Only or mainly English	
Welsh	81	19	100
Welsh and English	33	67	100
English	8	92	100

(n=288)

This pattern of language use appears to have been institutionalized at an early age.

Table 7 Language used with friends in the community when at primary school, by language of peer group (%)

Language used with friends in community while at primary school:	Language of present group of friends:		Total
	Only or mainly Welsh	Only or mainly English	
Welsh	81	19	100
Welsh and English	42	58	100
English	2	98	100

(n=288)

Those who had used mostly or only Welsh within their peer group when they were at primary school tended to be involved in current networks of friends which used mostly or only Welsh. A similar pattern was seen for the use of English. The patterns were identical when the use of language during school break times was observed.

A comparison of the language which the respondent uses with five named friends, compared with the language used by those friends among themselves, is indicative of the language allegiance of the individual and the impact of the network as a whole on language use. That is, whereas the individual may use one language with those friends he or she has named, it may well be that the named friends use a different language with one another.

The data indicated that when the respondent spoke Welsh with his or her friends, in 85 per cent of cases the friends also spoke only or mainly Welsh to each other; conversely, when the respondent spoke English, 89 per cent of those friends spoke only or mainly English to each other.

Table 8 Language predominantly used by present group of friends by language of the respondents with friends (%)

Language used by respondent with friends:	Language of present group of friends:		Total
	Only or mainly Welsh	Only or mainly English	
Only or mainly Welsh	85	15	100
Only or mainly English	11	89	100

(n=288)

Family Networks

There was a close correspondence between the language of the home and the language of the family network, and also the density of these networks was high, as would be expected. Again, not unexpectedly, the determining factor here was the language of the respondents' home.

Therefore those who used Welsh at home tended to use Welsh with the extended family, and similarly in the case of English.

Table 9 Language of extended family interactions by home language (%)

Home language:	Language of extended family interactions:		Total
	Only or mainly Welsh	Only or mainly English	
Welsh	94	6	100
Welsh and English	36	64	100
English	5	95	100

(n=288)

Community Networks

The young people in the sample varied quite substantially in the range and frequency of their community network contacts. These contacts typically included neighbours; people involved in service delivery (e.g. shopkeepers, post, milk); sports clubs such as skating, hockey, football, swimming; social and arts clubs such as the drama club, orchestra, choir and dance classes; as well as youth groups like young farmers' clubs, Scouts, the Urdd (Welsh youth movement); and religious institutions. Again a link between the language of the home and that of the community contacts was observed.

Table 10 Language of community interactions by home language (%)

Home language:	Language of community interactions:		Total
	Only or mainly Welsh	Only or mainly English	
Welsh	74	26	100
Welsh and English	43	57	100
English	28	74	100

(n=288)

Social Clubs

Around one-third of the respondents who were second-language Welsh speakers or had an understanding only of the language did not belong to any social clubs, whereas 95 per cent of fluent Welsh speakers belonged to one or more social clubs.

Furthermore, there was evidence of language polarization in the context of local clubs, depending upon the home language of the respondents, with 75 per cent of those whose home language was Welsh belonging to Welsh-language clubs, while 85 per cent of those from English-speaking homes belonged to clubs where the main or only language of interaction was English. Two-thirds of those from a bilingual home background belonged to clubs where the main or only language of interaction was English.

Table 11 Language of social club interactions by home language (%)

Home language:	Language of club interaction:		Total
	Only or mainly Welsh	Only or mainly English	
Welsh	75	25	100
Welsh and English	38	62	100
English	15	85	100

(n=288)

Furthermore, those with a mainly English-speaking network were less likely to be involved in social clubs than those with Welsh-speaking networks.

Table 12 Membership of social clubs by the language of the respondents' overall networks (%)

	Language of overall network:	
Membership of clubs:	Only or mainly Welsh	Only or mainly English
0	6	19
1	16	41
2	30	23
> 2	48	19
Total	100	100

(n=284)

Diary Evidence

The evidence which was collected through the diaries kept by each of the respondents made it clear that most of the time of the various respondents was spent in the company of their family, and their peer group/school friends. However, this does not mean that the community and clubs did not also exert an influence regarding which of the two languages is the normative language in which context. Obviously, those from homes where Welsh was either not used, or where it could not be used, were restricted in the extent that they used Welsh. Such families had their own network configurations as families, and these networks invariably focused on the use of English. Such group networks overlapped with the networks of the individual members. The extent to which each situational setting involving clubs, the community and the family reinforced the general pattern of language use played an important role in the institutionalization process.

In Bala, Pwllheli, Llandysul/Cardigan, Llanrwst and Machynlleth, the respondents from Welsh-speaking home backgrounds had mainly Welsh-speaking networks of friends, and those friends also used Welsh extensively among themselves. By contrast, in Amlwch, Ystradgynlais, Ammanford and Fishguard, the use of the Welsh language in the peer group was low. Among those respondents who came from an English-speaking home background, the use of Welsh within the peer group network was generally low, ranging from 0 per cent for Fishguard to 50 per cent for Bala.

Table 13 Rank order of incidence of use of Welsh in social networks by home language (%)

Location:	Percentage use of Welsh in social networks, where the home language is Welsh	Location:	Percentage use of Welsh in social networks, where the home language is English
Bala	94	Bala	50
Pwllheli	88	Pwllheli	47
Machynlleth	77	Lampeter	35
Llanrwst	76	Llangefni	25
Llandysul/Cardigan	75	Aberystwyth	20
Llangefni	60	Llandysul/Cardigan	16
Aberystwyth	59	Machynlleth	10
Lampeter	58	Llanrwst	9
Amlwch	27	Amlwch	9
Ammanford	8	Ammanford	5
Ystradgynlais	6	Ystradgynlais	1
Fishguard	2	Fishguard	0

Taking these two sets of data together, Bala and Pwllheli ranked highest on both measures. Machynlleth, Llandysul/Cardigan and Llanrwst stood out as having high and low figures for each measure (see Figure 1).

The implication of this comparison is, firstly, that those locations where respondents were from non-Welsh-speaking homes but had a relatively high use of Welsh within the peer network are the locations where there is greatest pressure for friends to conform by using Welsh as the normative practice. Secondly, there were locations where there was high use of Welsh within the peer network among the respondents from Welsh-speaking homes, and low use of Welsh within the peer networks of those from English-speaking homes; these communities had two quite distinct and separate language groups. Thirdly, there were locations where there was a low use of the Welsh language among both sets of peer groups, and in these communities the Welsh context was rapidly being assimilated into the English norm.

There were also some cases where the use of Welsh was low among respondents from Welsh-speaking homes, while there was a relatively

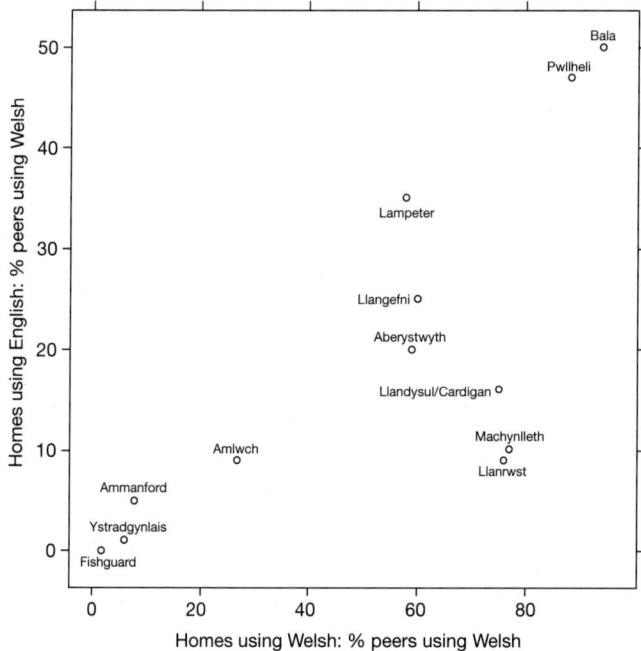

Figure 1 Incidence of use of Welsh among friends by home language

high use of Welsh among those from English-speaking homes. These were communities where Welsh could be treated as the norm, but which had sufficient salience to incorporate new members into the Welsh-language group. Language prestige or the value of language for social mobility probably played a role here.

There were some localities where respondents had kinship networks which used Welsh, even though they themselves came from non-Welsh-speaking homes. This was indicative of those who, for one reason or another, had opted to use English as the home language despite having local kinship roots – Fishguard, Amlwch and Llangefni stood out in this respect.

The data belonging to the community segment showed the extent to which Welsh remained the normative language for the community. In Bala, Llandysul/Cardigan, Pwllheli, Llanrwst and Machynlleth, there were similar patterns of Welsh-language use within the community and the peer group networks of those respondents from

Welsh-speaking homes. This meant that each segment reinforced the other in the use of Welsh, and it is this tendency for reinforcement from one institution to the other that is the essence of language normativity. Elsewhere, the use of Welsh in the community segment tended to be higher than that for the peer group for those from non-Welsh-speaking homes. This implied that those respondents lived in communities which used a significant amount more Welsh than they did themselves. There were also communities such as Fishguard, Ammanford and Amlwch where the use of Welsh within the community segment was low, and these were communities where the peer group had rejected Welsh.

The picture was similar for the segment on social clubs. For those from Welsh-speaking homes, the use of Welsh within this particular segment paralleled that found in the peer group and the community. In some cases, most notably Fishguard and Amlwch, they were considerably higher, which implied that the clubs did impose pressure on these respondents to use Welsh. The same cannot be said for those from non-Welsh-speaking homes, except perhaps in Llandysul/Cardigan and Machynlleth. Pwllheli also stood out in having far lower figures of Welsh-language use in the social clubs segment than for the peer group segment among those from non-Welsh-speaking homes. However, it is possible that these figures were heavily influenced by the number who did not associate with any local clubs and institutions.

Conclusions

The information produced in this study demonstrated that the linguistic nature of the home area of young people was a significant factor in the opportunities they had to use Welsh socially. There was an indication of a threefold typology of language communities based on the relationship between members of two different language groups.

Type 1: Assimilating communities

These were communities where there was considerable pressure on those who had not learned Welsh through family socialization to use the language. This pressure existed within the peer group, the community and the local clubs. They tended to be communities where the incidence of Welsh-language competence was high, and where the local community had not been entirely engulfed by recent in-migration. There was a single secondary school which socialized the pupils within what was largely a Welsh-language environment. This carried over into the community, where peer group socialization was not obliged to adapt to the existence of contemporaries who had attended schools with different language socialization patterns.

Cases: Pwllheli, Bala, Llandysul/Cardigan, Llangefni.

Type 2: Distinctive language groups

These were communities where Welsh speakers belonged to quite distinctive language groups and communities. On the one hand, those from homes which used Welsh, and even some from homes which used only English, belonged to a social world which focused on the use of Welsh in very much the same way as those in the communities associated with Type 1 above. On the other hand, most of those from homes which did not use Welsh, and some from homes which did use Welsh, belonged to a different social world within which the use of Welsh was rare. There were clubs which focused exclusively on the use of English, and communities where a large proportion of the population did not have any Welsh-language competence. The two communities may well occupy quite different geographical locations, but on the other hand they may coexist in the same location.

Cases: Llanrwst, Machynlleth, Lampeter, Aberystwyth.

Type 3: Assimilated communities

Finally, there were those type of localities where the Welsh-language group was rapidly becoming assimilated into the normative context where English was the predominant language. It appeared that for the vast majority, the school was the primary agency of Welsh-language use. Yet the peer group used virtually no Welsh, even among those whose home language was Welsh. The community and clubs continued to use Welsh, but to a much lesser degree than in the other locations. Furthermore, the density of Welsh in these segments for those from homes where English was used was very low. These tended to be locations where there had been a significant influx of in-migrants in recent years.

Cases: Amlwch, Fishguard, Ystradgynlais, Ammanford.

The information obtained from this study may be used to formulate language-planning initiatives not only of a general nature, but those which also focus on the types of language communities identified. However, it is necessary to recognize the limitations of such work: the findings for each community studied are primarily of relevance to action within those communities themselves. The evidence indicates that there is a need to increase the number of situations where the use of Welsh is normative. As well as increasing opportunities for young people to use Welsh in leisure activities, supporting and maintaining the significant social institutions that reinforce Welsh in community life, particularly in schools and their associated extracurricular Welsh medium activities, is essential.

Notes

[1] The study was carried out by the Centre for European Research (Wales) and Cwmni Iaith on behalf of the Welsh Language Board. The report was published in 2006 by the Board (see details in the References section). The author is grateful to the Welsh Language Board for permission to use the Report as the basis for this paper.
[2] 2001 Census: Main Statistics about Welsh, Welsh Language Board, issued on Welsh Language Board website 23 September 2003.

References

Welsh Assembly Government (2003). *Iaith Pawb: A National Action Plan for a Bilingual Wales*, Cardiff, Welsh Assembly Government.
Welsh Language Board (2006). *Young People's Social Networks and Language Use: Final Report*, Cardiff, Welsh Language Board.
Welsh Language Board, *2001 Census: Main Statistics about Welsh*, Welsh Language Board, issued on Welsh Language Board website 23 September 2003.
Welsh Language Board (2006). *The Welsh Language Board's Youth Strategy*, 2006.

Children's Acquisition of Welsh in a Bilingual Setting: A Psycholinguistic Perspective

Enlli Môn Thomas
College of Education and Life-Long Learning and
ESRC Centre for Bilingualism in Theory and Practice
Bangor University

and

Robert Mayr
Cardiff School of Health Sciences
University of Wales Institute Cardiff

Introduction

One of the most fascinating aspects of language acquisition is the young infant's ability to transform their developing knowledge of the complex underpinnings of language into overt expressions of speech. In the first three years of life, they are able to participate successfully in communicative interactions, producing language that mirrors that of their environment. At that stage, they will not only have learned to produce individual word forms that approximate those of the language(s) they are learning, but also to combine them to form two- and three-word expressions. Eventually, the child who was initially only able to utter a few indistinct sounds is able to communicate his or her desired message in a language-appropriate and meaningful way.

How children achieve linguistic competence is still a matter of debate. Whilst it is generally accepted that children are equipped with an in-built 'aid' to language learning that enables the development of human speech, theorists disagree about the exact nature of this aid. Likewise, whilst many researchers agree that such an aid must interact in some way with the linguistic input from the environment in order to allow children to acquire the language spoken around them, theorists disagree in respect of the precise role assumed by the input in the acquisition process (Hoff, 2001; Gathercole and Hoff, 2007).

Language acquisition research falls broadly into two major camps, each of which has offered its own distinct set of explanations.[1] Those favouring the *nativist* or *generative* theoretical position, as represented by Chomsky's theory of *Transformational Grammar* (Chomsky, 1957), and his most recent influential modification, *Minimalism* (Chomsky, 1995), support the notion that the child is innately endowed with linguistic knowledge in the form of *Universal Grammar* (UG). According to this view, language constitutes an evolutionary adaptation in *homo sapiens*, a 'language instinct' (Pinker, 1984) that manifests itself in a domain-specific module in the mind which is independent of general cognition (Fodor, 1983). Innate linguistic knowledge facilitates the language-acquisition process, which, apart from lexical learning, is said to involve no more than a process of setting the linguistic 'parameters' relevant to the input language received.

Those favouring a *cognitive* approach to language-acquisition theory, as represented in *usage-based* accounts (e.g., Tomasello, 2000a, b; 2003), *Constructivism* (e.g., Gathercole, 2007), *Connectionism* (e.g., Elman et al., 1996), and the *Competition Model* (Bates and MacWhinney, 1989), among others, support the notion that children approach the language-learning process devoid of language, equipped instead with an innate set of general cognitive processes that aid their interpretation, processing, and storage of linguistic input. Language is therefore constructed from the input, is learned within the context of wider cognition, and takes place within the context of socio-cognitive relations with others (Tomasello, 2003). What the nativist and cognitive approaches have in common, then, is that they both assume some role for certain innate mechanisms, although they differ in terms of what these mechanisms may be.

These two conflicting positions allow for the formulation of different predictions about various aspects of the process of language acquisition. Three aspects of that process are explored in this chapter, with particular reference to Welsh. The first of these relates to the nature of the child's knowledge of language, the second to their rate of learning, and the third to the role of input.

Regarding the nature of the child's knowledge of language, nativists would argue that abstract linguistic structures are already present at birth in the form of *Universal Grammar*, as we have seen. Together with innate UG principles, minimal exposure to the language of the environment serves to trigger the setting of language-specific parameters. Children's knowledge of language is thus innately systematic, and very much rule-based (see e.g., Pinker, 1999). Under the cognitive approach, in contrast, abstract linguistic categories or structures are not simply 'present' at birth. Rather, children's grammars are assembled around individual items and combinations of these. For example, Tomasello (1992) has shown in his *Verb Island Hypothesis* that children use lexically specific patterns for different verbs, so that some verbs may be used in merely one type of construction (e.g., Eat X), while others may be used in several (e.g., Drink; Drink X; Drink to X, etc.). Children's developing knowledge of language, according to the cognitive account, is thus piecemeal and item-based.

On the rate of learning, nativists would argue that language 'develops... without conscious effort or formal instruction... [and] is qualitatively the same in every individual' (Pinker, 1994: 4–5). Children need only receive the smallest amount of exposure to the language of their environment in order to 'trigger' structural learning of the language. Once triggered, the process of selecting the relevant sets of rules that are appropriate for the language being learnt is assumed to be rapid and largely error-free. The cognitive position, on the other hand, suggests that the process of language learning is protracted and error-marked, reflecting much of the child's construction of their own grammar. Individually learnt items are gradually pieced together emerging at a much later stage as a grammar of an abstract and systematically organized description (Tomasello, 2000a, b).

Finally, concerning input, whilst both accounts agree that input does play a role in language acquisition, they differ in how important they consider its role. Since children learn language in the absence of formal teaching or corrective feedback, nativists view the role of input as minimal, necessary only inasmuch as it helps identify the linguistic system spoken to the child and to trigger parameter-setting (Weissenborn, Goodluck and Roeper, 1992). The linguistic input a child receives is not seen as having much influence on the actual end-product achieved (Bialystok, 2001). The cognitive account, on the other hand, sees language learning (like any form of learning) as a largely input-driven process: 'language ... is constructed by the child using inborn mental equipment but operating on information provided by the environment' (Hoff, 2001: 15) (see Gathercole and Hoff, 2007 for a thorough account of the role of input in language learning).

This chapter reviews some recent studies of children's acquisition of Welsh, and will address the following core questions: (1) What is the nature of Welsh-speaking children's knowledge of the complex system they are learning? Is it systematic and rule-based (nativist), or piecemeal and item-by-item (cognitive)? (2) What is their rate of learning? Is it rapid and error-free (nativist), or protracted, and erroneous (cognitive)? Since Welsh is spoken in a bilingual setting, it is also possible to explore the processes of learning a minority language under conditions of restricted input. We will therefore address a third question: (3) What role does the amount of exposure play in bilingual children's acquisition of complex systems in Welsh? Does it play a minimal role (nativist), or does greater input facilitate earlier acquisition (cognitive)? Such explorations have wide-reaching implications for policy-related issues and language-planning strategies in Wales and beyond.

Complex Systems of Welsh: Mutation and Gender

Mutation in Welsh

Welsh, like the other Celtic languages, operates a process of *mutation* – a set of morpho-phonological changes that usually affect the initial consonants of words. Traditionally, there are three types of mutation processes in Welsh: Soft Mutation (SM) (often called 'Lenition'); Aspirate Mutation (AM) (often called 'Spirant Mutation'); and Nasal Mutation (NM). We will restrict our discussion here to SM and AM.

Under SM, the voiceless stops (/p, t, k/) and liquids (/ɬ, r̥/) become voiced (/b, d, g, l, r/), the voiced stops (/b, d/) and the labial nasal (/m/) become fricatives (/v, ð, v/) and /g/ is deleted. Under AM, the voiceless stops (/p, t, k/) become fricatives (/f, θ, x/).[2]

Although these sound alternations are phonological in the sense that they result in phonological change, mutations are not triggered by phonological factors (although, originally, phonological alternations were phonetically conditioned – see Jackson, 1959; Watkins 1961, 1993), but by various morpho-syntactic environments (Tallerman, 1990). Most of these 'triggers' for mutation are lexical (i.e., the mutation is triggered by a particular word – e.g., demonstrative verbs, some prepositions, and certain numerals trigger SM; certain conjunctions and prepositions trigger AM), although some are purely syntactic (i.e., the mutation is applied to a word when it occurs in a particular syntactic position – e.g., direct objects of personal verbs) (see Ball and Müller, 1992).

Learning how to apply mutation rules is not a simple case of identifying a trigger and applying the appropriate sound change to a target. The Welsh mutation system is fraught with irregularities (see Thomas and Gathercole, 2007), and, in colloquial speech, there is considerable variation in adherence to the mutations, even in adult speech (e.g., Ball, 1988; Thomas, 1984; Watkins, 1993; Jones, 1998).

Grammatical gender in Welsh

Grammatical gender systems are either transparent or opaque. In 'transparent' systems, such as those found in Spanish, Italian, or Hebrew, the gender of a noun can often be inferred on the basis of its form. In opaque languages, in contrast, this is not the case and the assignment of a noun to a particular gender is often arbitrary.

In Welsh, the initial consonant sound of feminine singular nouns undergoes SM after the definite article *y(r)* 'the' and after the numeral *un* 'one' – *y gath* < *cath* 'the cat' (fem.), vs. *y ci* < *ci* 'the dog' (masc.). Adjectives that are used nominally in place of feminine singular nouns (*y fechan* < *bechan* 'the little (girl)') may also undergo SM in this context (Tallerman, 1987). The initial consonant sounds of adjectives (or nouns behaving adjectivally) also undergo SM when modifying feminine singular nouns: *cath ddu* < *du* 'black cat' vs. *ci du* < *du* 'black dog'.

Grammatical gender is also shown in distant reference to the noun in the form of pronouns and possessives, which must agree with the gender of the antecedent noun. For example, the feminine gender of the (homonymic) possessive adjective *ei* 'his/her/its' is marked by AM on the modified word (*mae'r ddafad wedi disgyn ar **ei phen** < pen* 'the sheep has fallen on her/its head', ***ei thrwyn** < trwyn* 'her/its nose', ***ei choes** < coes* 'her/its leg'). The masculine gender of the same form is marked by SM on the modified word (e.g., *mae'r mochyn wedi disgyn* *ar ei ben* < *pen* 'the pig has fallen on his/its head', *ei drwyn* < *trwyn* 'his/its nose', *ei goes* < *coes* 'his/its leg'). Although these distant forms are applied to animate and inanimate nouns, the extent to which inanimate nouns are marked for gender in this way in colloquial speech is unclear (see, e.g., Jones, 1993; Jones, 1998, for Welsh; Dorian, 1976, for Scottish Gaelic).

Together, these systems provide an excellent basis from which to explore the three core theoretical questions outlined in this paper. This is for a number of reasons. First, they are highly complex systems that allow for the experimental manipulation of their structural features in ways that permit exploration of the *nature* of children's knowledge of the system. Second, since they are pervasive systems within the language, it is possible to follow their developmental trajectories across time, and to subsequently map their *rate* of development. Third, they are structures that are learnt by children who are also learning English. However, the amount of time a bilingual Welsh-English child spends exposed to each language will vary from child to child. Studying the acquisition of these structures across different types of Welsh-English bilinguals allows for the exploration of the role of *input* (in terms of amount of exposure) in the acquisition process.

The next section reviews recent studies of Welsh alongside other cross-linguistic studies. The results of these studies are interpreted in relation to the specific predictions expressed by the two contrasting theoretical positions and in relation to the three core questions outlined above.

Research evidence

1 The nature of children's knowledge of language

How do we know how children's knowledge of language is represented in the mind? One method involves looking at what children do when they are given a novel word that they have never heard before (e.g., Berko, 1958). If they are able to modify the word consistently with the underlying rules of the grammar – without ever having been exposed to the 'creative' new use of the new word – and thus demonstrate productive use of the rule, then one could argue that the child is working from an abstract linguistic structure that allows him or her to be creative (within the confines of the grammar). Such behaviour would suggest systematic learning. If, however, children are unable to modify the novel word appropriately (given the syntactic context), even when given a number of cues to the grammatical status of the context, this would suggest that the child is not basing his or her knowledge on an underlying abstract grammar. The child must, instead, be learning item by item (Tomasello, 2000a). In the following, empirical studies addressing the nature of children's linguistic knowledge will be reviewed separately for mutation and gender.

Mutation

Studies on the acquisition of Welsh mutation have shown that the three different mutation types are not acquired simultaneously, but that SM is acquired before AM and NM (Thomas and Gathercole, 2007; Jones, 1992). Furthermore, some triggers are acquired earlier and with more ease than others, both within and across mutation types (Hatton, 1988; Ball, 1984; Davies, 1984). For example, Hatton (1988) found that NM after the possessive adjective *fy* 'my' developed between ages seven and nine, reaching an established pattern of use by age ten. However, it was not until age ten that the initial development of NM occurred after the preposition *yn* 'in' (possibly due to the fact that *yn* is a homonymic form that also triggers SM as a predicative particle). Therefore, an established pattern of use of NM seems to develop in the context of *fy* + NM by the age of ten, but not until after that age in the context of *yn* + NM.

Thomas and Gathercole (2007) also found that within SM performance was better with feminine nouns than with masculine nouns. That is, when SM was triggered by the prepositions *ar* 'on' and *o* 'from, (out) of', children tended to mutate feminine nouns significantly more often than they mutated masculine nouns. Children seem to know something about the frequency of occurrence of SM with feminine forms that makes it easier to use SM with feminine rather than with masculine forms in these contexts, indicating more 'statistical' (frequency-based) than systematic (rule-based) learning.

Finally, some of the data indicate that children are acquiring specific forms for particular nouns. For example, Bellin (1984) reported that children learning Welsh as a second language were less likely to mutate some borrowed items (*cap* 'cap' and *tê* 'tea'), suggesting that Welsh-speaking children's progression may be from the basic to the mutated form. Similar data from Breton and Irish indicate children's initial learning as having a single form per noun (Stephens, 1996; Ó Baoill, 1992).[3]

Together, these studies support the cognitivists' notion that children approach the mutation system in a piecemeal, item-by-item manner.

Gender

Recent studies have explored children's acquisition of grammatical gender in Welsh (e.g., Thomas 2001, Gathercole et al. 2001, Gathercole and Thomas 2005, Thomas and Gathercole, 2007). These studies provided cues to the gender status of nouns (both real and novel nouns) to see whether children make use of those cues to ascertain the gender of the noun and to show their understanding by marking the same noun for its gender in a different context elsewhere.

Given the complexity of the system, it is not surprising that the results from these studies do not demonstrate systematic, rule-based knowledge of the Welsh grammatical gender system. Instead, children show a piecemeal, item-by-item route to acquiring gender constructs, sometimes performing better on some constructs than on others. In Thomas (2001, 2007) and Thomas and Gathercole (2007), neither children nor adults performed any better when there was a cue than when there was no cue. Gathercole and Thomas (2005) noted that although cues seemed to aid children's performance in places, this was not across the board, and sometimes these cues had the reverse effect. For example, word-form cues (e.g., nouns ending in *-en, -es, -wraig*) seemed to be useful only for nouns for humans and inanimate objects, not animals.

Other data support item-based learning of Welsh gender. For example, Gathercole and Thomas (2005) found that children were better able to: (1) mark gender in local constructs on real than on novel nouns, (2) mark gender on nouns for human referents better than on nouns for animal or inanimate referents, and (3) perform differently on native vs. borrowed vocabulary. They also found better performance on the identification of the correct pronoun (63.2 per cent correct) than on the identification of the correct form after *ei* 'his/her/its' in long-distant gender constructs (59.7 per cent). Children are clearly learning various aspects of the system at different times and build their knowledge of the system around individual items.

When linguistic systems are as complex as the grammatical gender system in Welsh, lacking consistency between form and meaning, and tending to be variable in the input, children (and adults) may rely on additional cues to gender, in the form of semantic information, in order to help interpret the gender of a noun. This may be why Welsh-speaking children and adults, as a general trend, perform better on nouns for humans than on nouns for animals and inanimate objects in studies of gender (e.g., Gathercole et al. 2001; Gathercole and Thomas 2005) (although see Jones, 1998, and Thomas and Gathercole, 2005, for additional discussions relating to structural change). The next section explores the rate at which children learn these systems.

2 Rate of learning

Contrary to research indicating rapid and easy acquisition of linguistic structures in general (e.g., Pinker, 1994), and that of grammatical gender in particular (e.g., Szagun, Stumper, Sondag, and Franik, 2007), other empirical studies indicate that certain structures are not learned until much later in development and that the acquisition process is protracted and error-marked (e.g., Nippold, 1998). In the following section, the evidence from mutation and gender studies in Welsh is discussed.

Mutation

Experimental data indicate that the acquisition of mutation is not complete until well after age five (Bellin, 1984, 1988). Some studies even suggest that the system is still in the process of acquisition after age nine (Gathercole et al., 2001; Thomas, 2001, 2007; Thomas and Gathercole, 2007), or even age eleven (Hatton, 1988; Jones, 1992; Gathercole and Thomas, 2005). For example, Thomas and Gathercole (2007) showed that nine-year-old children were still in the process of acquiring SM after some prepositions, despite the fact they were all L1 speakers of Welsh and attending Welsh-medium schools. However, their performance did continue to approach the adult norm across the ages, indicative of a slow learning process being in place (see Figure 1). This was in contrast to their performance on AM, which indicated no development with age (see Figure 2).

These data suggest, therefore, that children are learning SM and AM separately, and at different times. Whereas children are still progressing with their use of SM at age nine years, it seems that children's development of AM in non-gendered contexts is more static.

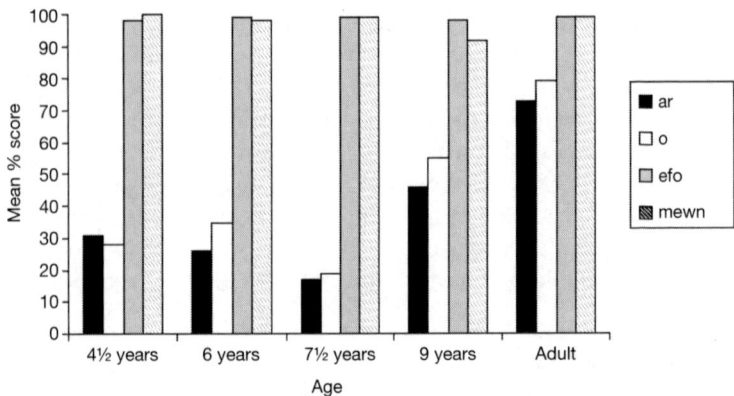

Figure 1 Children's and adults' performance on triggers to SM (*ar* 'on' and *o* 'from/(out) of') and non-triggering contexts (*efo* 'with' and *mewn* 'in'). (Adapted from Thomas and Gathercole, 2007.)

Gender

In addition to demonstrating an ability to make use of the formal regularities of the gender systems they are learning, many studies have also demonstrated that children do this at a very young age. For example, Levy (1983) noted that gender-marked plurals appeared first in Hebrew-speaking children's speech at 1;10. By the age of 3 years, children begin to show understanding of the phonological regularities of the final noun syllable that determines the choice of the plural suffix (i.e., nouns ending in /a/ or /t/ are feminine and take {-ot} as their plural suffix ending; other nouns take {-im} in the plural).

More recently, however, studies of Welsh (and other gendered languages that have opaque grammatical gender systems) have demonstrated a more protracted route to acquisition. For Welsh, at least, it is not until after age nine that children begin to demonstrate an increased awareness of gender categories, and they are yet to approach the adult 'norm', even at that age.

The most compelling evidence comes from Gathercole and Thomas (2005). In one study they presented 306 bilingual Welsh-English children from various home-language backgrounds (only Welsh, Welsh and English, only English) across various age groups

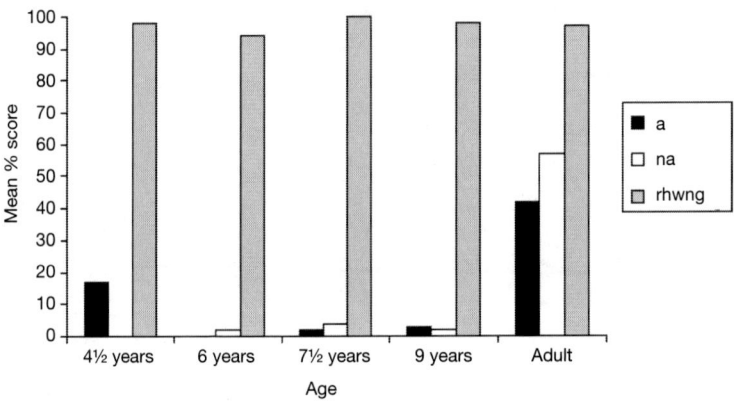

Figure 2 Children's and adults' performance on triggers to AM (*a* 'and' and *na* 'nor') and non-triggering contexts (*rhwng* 'between'). (Adapted from Thomas and Gathercole, 2007.)

(roughly 3, 5, 7 and 9 years) with a forced-choice picture-card task. Each card included two pictures, one involving the referent of a feminine noun, the other involving the referent of a masculine noun. The experimenter introduced the picture with a sentence containing a masculine and a feminine noun – e.g., *Roedd y ddysgl las* (fem.) *a'r blodyn piws* (masc.) *ar y bwrdd* 'the blue dish and the purple flower were on the table'. The child was then shown the same two pictures slightly modified, and heard a second sentence that included either a masculine or a feminine pronoun, or the masculine or feminine *ei* – e.g., *Ond nath o dorri* 'but it (masc.) broke' or *ond nath hi dorri* 'but it (fem.) broke'. The child's task was to select which picture corresponded best with the sentence they heard.

The results revealed that although there was a general progression with age, parts of the system were mastered at earlier ages than others. Masculine and feminine pronouns denoting humans were selected appropriately by ages five or seven (age five for children from only-Welsh-speaking homes – 85.6 per cent and Welsh-and-English-speaking homes – 81 per cent; and age seven for children from only English-speaking homes – 79.1 per cent). However, other parts of the system – e.g., feminine *ei* – created particular difficulty for children from only-English-speaking homes at all ages, and inanimate forms seemed to cause difficulty for all children at all ages. It may be that children take a very long time to learn the gender distinctions for nouns for non-human referents as they rely somewhat on semantic information to help decide the gender of a noun.

What these results suggest is that when a language involves a gender system that offers no clear indication of noun gender, any 'late' development or apparent 'lack' of systematic knowledge of the system may be attributable to its complexity. It may also, in part, be influenced by adult use of these systems, and, as the results above suggest, by levels of input. The final section looks at the role of input in acquiring these systems.

3 Amount of input

According to the nativist position, only minimal input is required to trigger the language-acquisition process, as we have seen. However, in contrast to this position, several studies have shown that the amount of input that children receive directly affects their attainment levels (e.g., Hart and Risley, 1995; Oller and Eilers, 2002). For example, the studies reported in Oller and Eilers (2002) include a variety of measures of children's abilities in English and in Spanish. Across all tasks and all studies, the general pattern to emerge was that the more input the child received in a particular language, the better they performed in that language. The authors argued that bilingual children take longer to acquire the 'critical mass' of exposure to certain linguistic structures that is necessary in order for them to acquire a productive grasp of their stored knowledge. These studies therefore support the notion that the greater the amount of exposure, the quicker and 'fuller' the acquisition, indicating a specific and important role for input, as the cognitivists would argue. The role of input in studies of mutation and gender in Welsh will be discussed below.

Mutation

The amount and type of linguistic input a child receives has been shown to influence mutation use by children in Welsh. Children whose parents are not L1 speakers seem to be less productive with some triggers to mutation than those of L1 parents (Hatton, 1988; Bellin, 1988). However, some L2 children may perform 'better' than L1 children on some of the less consistent triggers (e.g., *yn* 'in' for NM), reflecting an effect of the difference in acquisition styles. Whilst the L2 child acquires Welsh largely in a formal setting (through Welsh lessons at school), L1 speakers, on the other hand, may acquire Welsh more naturalistically and reflect the more colloquial (and often non-standard) usages in such tasks (Davies 1982).

Children's performance can also vary according to the style of conversing (e.g., Bellin, 1988) and the type of test (e.g., Davies, 1982; Hatton, 1988). These differences are again related to the child's experience and exposure to language: tests that elicit formal linguistic expression may better match the L2-background speaker of Welsh, allowing them to reflect a classroom language model more than a vernacular model like the L1 speakers.

In his study of five- to nine-year-old children's productive command of mutation, Bellin (1988) found that children from only-Welsh-speaking homes in Wales and those living in London (attending the Welsh-medium school in the city) outperformed those living in Wales but with non-Welsh-speaking parents, although performances improved with age for all groups. He further noted that children from non-Welsh-speaking home backgrounds were more reluctant to integrate borrowed items into the mutation system than children from Welsh-speaking homes. It may well be that these children had yet to acquire the 'critical mass' of exposure to these forms that is necessary to help generalize across items. What is clear is that all children from all language backgrounds need to hear as much use of mutation as possible in formal and informal settings in order for it to emerge, at a later stage, as a systematically organized system.

Gender

Recent studies suggest that the more Welsh a child receives as part of his or her linguistic input, the more likely they are to mark gender distinctions in their speech. Children who hear the most Welsh show an understanding of gender distinctions earlier than those who have yet to acquire enough 'critical mass' of exposure to the language that will allow them to 'sort through' the irregularities of the system.

For example, Gathercole and Thomas (2005) conducted a semi-naturalistic production task with 324 children across four age groups (roughly 3, 5, 7 and 9 years), who were from one of three home language groups (only Welsh at home, Welsh and English at home, only English at home), attending either Welsh-medium or bilingual Welsh-English schools. The children were asked to describe a series of cartoons using a sentence structure that contained a definite article *y(r)* ('the'), an adjective, and the possessive adjective *ei* 'his/her/its' + mutation – e.g., *aeth y gath goch i mewn i focs, a dangos ei chlust* (went-the-cat-red-into-box-and-show-its-ear) 'the red cat went into (a) box and showed its ear'. Each sentence was recorded, analysed and scored in relation to whether the child marked the noun appropriately for its gender. The results revealed that the more Welsh the children received on a daily basis, the better their performance in the test. In general, children from only-Welsh-speaking homes performed better than the other children, but those from mixed Welsh- and English-speaking homes also outperformed those from only English-speaking homes on some forms. This meant that children with at least some Welsh in the home progressed towards the performance levels of those from only-Welsh-speaking homes, but at a slower rate (i.e., showing improved performance by age nine). Also, the more Welsh instruction received at school, the better the performance on marking the adjective on nouns for humans and on producing SM after *ei* to mark the masculine form.

In terms of receptive ability, results from a second study reported in Gathercole and Thomas (2005) highlighted further differences in performance across different exposure patterns to Welsh. For example, performance on the interpretation of pronouns in relation to human antecedents was good in children from only-Welsh- and mixed Welsh- and English-speaking homes by age five, and by age seven in children from only-English-speaking homes. Moreover, when the possessive adjective *ei* was in reference to a feminine human antecedent, requiring the production of AM, children from only Welsh-speaking homes performed well by age five, those from mixed Welsh and English homes performed well by age seven, whereas those from only English-speaking homes showed no progression with age, and performed poorly in general on this construct. This again indicates that, as far as complex structures are concerned, the amount of exposure a child receives in relation to these structures contributes to the child's acquisition of these structures, and the extent to which they obtain a productive grasp of their stored knowledge of the system.

Conclusion

This chapter examined three key questions regarding children's acquisition of language. They concerned the nature of children's linguistic knowledge (systematic or item-based), the rate at which they gain this knowledge (rapid and error-free, or protracted and error-marked), and the role the amount of input received plays in bilingual children's language acquisition (minimal or essential role). Using recent evidence from studies of children's acquisition of mutation and grammatical gender in Welsh, the answers to these questions were interpreted in light of the predictions afforded by the two key theoretical positions presented at the beginning of the chapter, i.e. the nativist and cognitivist accounts.

In answer to the first question regarding the nature of the child's knowledge of language, performance in non-gendered mutation contexts seems to be linked to the type of mutation involved, the specific trigger involved, and the gender of the noun. Performance in gender tasks reveals different performance on nouns for humans vs. nouns for animals and inanimate objects; a general lack of ability to generalize the gender rule to novel items; irregular use of cues to help identify the gender status of nouns; and a general lack of awareness of agreement between the various markers of gender. There is no systematic rule-based understanding of the system evident: children (and adults) do not draw on the potential links between different gender-marked constructs in order to generate an abstract, rule-based representation of the system. Rather, children approach the system in a more piecemeal, context-by-context fashion. This supports the predictions laid out by the cognitive perspective in relation to item-based learning of the system.

In answer to the second question regarding the rate of learning, children are still in the process of acquiring the Welsh mutation system and the gender system even at age nine. Whilst the more transparent aspects of the system are acquired a little earlier (e.g., pronouns referring to humans by age five or seven), this is still relatively old in comparison to studies that are cited in support of quick and effortless learning. This evidence supports the notion that language takes a long time to master, and that the acquisition of complex structures is not entirely straightforward. These results support the cognitive theoretical position and the notion that the process of language learning is not always complete by the age of four years.

In answer to the third question, input, in terms of amount of exposure, plays a crucial role in Welsh-speaking children's acquisition of complex structures. The more input children receive in Welsh at home and at school, the quicker and better they master aspects of these systems in the spoken language. That there is a clear relationship between the amount of time a child spends hearing and using a particular language and their ultimate abilities with certain linguistic forms in that language provides further support for the principles underlying the cognitive assumption that language learning is largely input-driven.

Together, the evidence presented here from studies of children's acquisition of complex structures of Welsh, in combination with recent cross-linguistic evidence, provides strong support for the cognitivists' approach to language acquisition. Welsh-speaking children's acquisition of mutation and gender is protracted, error-marked, and very much item-based. When a language operates under natural conditions of reduced input due to the nature of bilingualism, the acquisition of complex constructs takes longer to master. Such results highlight the need for continued support towards the use of Welsh in schools and also in extracurricular activities if children are to acquire native-like proficiency in the language, and if Welsh, as a spoken language, is to continue to flourish in the twenty-first century.

Notes

[1] Note that the two positions outlined here constitute extreme positions. Other accounts have attempted to 'merge' these – e.g., Fisher (2002). However, a detailed discussion of these theories is beyond the scope of this chapter.

[2] Graphemically, <p, t, c, b, d, ll, rh, m> become <b, d, g, f, dd, l, r, f> under SM, and <p, t, c> become <ph, th, ch> under AM.

[3] Note that the mutated form is acquired first in Breton, most probably since it developed a definite article that also triggers mutation.

References

Ball, M. J. (1984). 'Sociolinguistic aspects of the Welsh mutation system', unpublished doctoral dissertation, University of Wales.

—— (ed.) (1988). *The Use of Welsh: A Contribution to Sociolinguistics*, Clevedon, Multilingual Matters.

Ball, M. J. and Müller, N. (1992). *Mutation in Welsh*, London, Routledge.

Bates, E. A. and MacWhinney, B. (1989). 'Functionalism and the competition model', in B. MacWhinney and E. A. Bates (eds.), *The Crosslinguistic*

Study of Sentence Processing, Cambridge, Cambridge University Press, pp. 3–73.
Bellin, W. (1984). 'Welsh phonology in acquisition', in M. J. Ball and G. E. Jones (eds.), *Welsh Phonology*, Cardiff, University of Wales Press.
—— (1988). 'The development of pronunciation', in Ball (1988).
Berko, J. (1958). 'The child's learning of English morphology', *Word*, 14, 150–77.
Bialystok, E. (2001). *Bilingualism in Development: Language, Literacy, and Cognition*, Cambridge, Cambridge University Press.
Chomsky, N (1957). *Syntactic Structures*, The Hague, Mouton.
—— (1995). *The Minimalist Programme*, Cambridge, Mass., MIT Press.
Davies, D. G. (1984). 'Mutating mutations?', *Cardiff Working Papers in Welsh Linguistics*, 3, 63–76.
Dorian, N. (1976). 'Gender in a terminal Gaelic dialect', *Scottish Gaelic Studies,* 12, 279–82.
Elman, J. L., Bates, E. A., Johnson, M. H., Karmiloff-Smith, A., Parisi, D. and Plunkett, K. (1996). *Rethinking Innateness: A Connectionist Perspective on Development*, Cambridge, Mass., MIT Press.
Fisher, C. (2002). 'The role of abstract syntactic knowledge in language acquisition: a reply to Tomasello', *Cognition*, 82, 259–78.
Fodor, J. A. (1983). *The Modularity of Mind*, Cambridge, Mass., MIT Press.
Gathercole, V. C. Mueller (2007). 'Miami and north Wales, so far and yet so near: Constructivist account of morpho-syntactic development in bilingual children', *International Journal of Bilingual Education and Bilingualism*, 10, 3, 224–47.
Gathercole, V. C. Mueller and Hoff, E. (2007). 'Input and the acquisition of language: three questions', in E. Hoff and M. Shatz (eds.), *Blackwell Handbook of Language Development*, Oxford, Blackwell.
Gathercole, V. C. Mueller and Thomas, E. M. (2005). 'Minority language survival: input factors influencing the acquisition of Welsh', in J. Cohen, K. T. McAlister, K. Rolstad and J. MacSwan (eds.), *Proceedings of the 4th International Symposium on Bilingualism*, Somerville, Cascadilla Press.
Gathercole, V. C. Mueller, Thomas, E. M. and Laporte, N. I. (2001). 'The acquisition of grammatical gender in Welsh', *Journal of Celtic Language Learning*, 6, 53–87.
Hart, B. and Risley, T. (1995). *Meaningful Differences in Everyday Experience of Young American Children*, Baltimore, Paul Brookes Publishing Co.
Hatton, L. (1988). 'The development of the nasal mutation in the speech of schoolchildren', in Ball (1988).
Hoff, E. (2001). *Language Development*, second edn, Belmont, Calif., Wadsworth.
Jackson, K. (1959). 'The dawn of the Welsh language', in A. J. Rodrick (ed.), *Wales through the Ages*, Llandybïe, Christopher Davies.
Jones, B. M. (1992). *Linguistic Performance and Language Background: A Study of Pupils in Welsh-Medium Schools*, Aberystwyth, Y Ganolfan Astudiaethau Addysg.

—— (1993). *Ar Lafar ac ar Bapur: Cyflwyniad i'r Berthynas Rhwng yr Iaith Lafar a'r Iaith Ysgrifenedig*, Aberystwyth, Y Ganolfan Astudiaethau Addysg.

Jones. M. C. (1998). *Language Obsolescence and Revitalization: Linguistic Change in Two Sociolinguistically Contrasting Welsh Communities*, Oxford, Clarendon Press.

Levy, Y. (1983). 'It's frogs all the way down', *Cognition*, 15, 75–93.

Nippold, M. A. (1998). *Later Language Development: The School-Age and Adolescent Years*, second edn, Austin, Tex, Pro-Ed.

Ó Baoill, D. (1992). 'Developmental stages in the acquisition of Irish phonology and initial mutations', in D. Ó Baoill (ed.), *The Acquisition of Irish as a First Language*, Dublin, IRAAL.

Oller, D. K. and Eilers, R. E. (2002). *Language and Literacy in Bilingual Children*, Clevedon, Multilingual matters.

Pinker, S. (1984). *Language Learnability and Language Development*, Cambridge, Mass., Harvard University Press.

—— (1994). *The Language Instinct*, London, Penguin Books.

—— (1999). *Words and Rules: The Ingredients of Language*, London, Phoenix.

Stephens, J. (1996). 'The acquisition of mutations in Breton', in *Lesser Used Languages: Project Work in Progress*, vol 2, Cardiff, University of Wales Institute.

Szagun, G., Stumper, B., Sondag, N., and Franik, M. (2007). 'The acquisition of gender marking by young German-speaking children: evidence for learning guided by phonological regularities', *Journal of Child Language*, 34, 445–71.

Tallerman, M. (1987). 'Mutation and the syntactic structure of modern colloquial Welsh', unpublished doctoral dissertation, University of Wales.

—— (1990). 'VSO word order and consonantal mutation in Welsh', *Linguistics*, 28, 1, 389–416.

Thomas, E. M. (2001). 'Aspects of gender mutation in Welsh', unpublished doctoral dissertation, University of Wales.

—— (2007). 'Natur prosesau caffael iaith gan blant: marcio cenedl enwau yn y Gymraeg', *Gwerddon*, 1, 58–94.

Thomas, E. M. and Gathercole, V. C. Mueller (2005). 'Obsolescence or survival for Welsh in the face of English dominance?', in J. Cohen, K. T. McAlister, K. Rolstad and J. MacSwan (eds.), *Proceedings of the 4th International Symposium on Bilingualism*, Somerville, Cascadilla Press.

—— (2007). 'Children's productive command of grammatical gender and mutation in Welsh: an alternative to rule-based learning', *First Language*, 27, 3, 251–78.

Thomas, P. W. (1984). 'Variation in South Glamorgan consonant mutation', in M. J. Ball and G. E. Jones (eds.), *Welsh Phonology*, Cardiff, University of Wales press.

Tomasello, M. (1992). *First Verbs: A Case Study of Early Grammatical Development*, Cambridge, Cambridge University Press.

—— (2000a). 'The item-based nature of children's early syntactic development', *Trends in Cognitive Sciences,* 4, 4, 156–63.
—— (2000b). 'Do young children have adult syntactic competence?', *Cognition*, 74, 209–53.
—— (2003). *Constructing a Language: A Usage-Based Theory of Language Acquisition*, Cambridge, Mass., Havard University Press.
Watkins, T. A. (1961). *Ieithyddiaeth: Agweddau ar Astudio Iaith*, Cardiff, University of Wales Press.
—— (1993). 'Welsh', in M. J. Ball and J. Fife (eds.), *The Celtic Languages*, London, Routledge.
Weissenborn, J., Goodluck, H., and Roeper, T. (1992). 'Introduction: old and new problems in the study of language acquisition', in J. Weissenborn, H. Goodluck, and T. Roeper (eds.), *Theoretical Issues in Language Acquisition: Continuity and Change in Development*, Hillsdale NJ, Erlbaum.

Welsh Speakers: Age Profile and Out-Migration

Hywel M. Jones

Introduction

The age profile of people reported by the Census as able to speak Welsh has changed substantially in recent decades. The pattern in which a lower percentage speaks Welsh in each generation has seemingly been halted, so that the percentage able to speak Welsh amongst school-age children is now much higher than the percentage able to speak Welsh in their parents' generation. A similar pattern can be seen too in the numbers, rather than percentages, of Welsh speakers. These changes reflect not only the effects of education but also changes to the composition of the population of Wales arising from migration, and rates of retention of the language once learnt. While this chapter builds on previous work examining the extent to which the young retain their ability in the language, its main focus is on the factors associated with out-migration.

Although the change in the age profile of Welsh speakers between 1991 and 2001 was remarkable, there had been a substantial change over the previous decade too. The numbers of Welsh speakers in their late teens or twenties recorded in Wales in 1991 was not what might have been expected on the basis of the 1981 figures and a similar pattern of loss was seen when comparing the 2001 results with the 1991 results (Figure 1).

The effects of education have been analysed previously (Jones, 2007a) as have language transition rates (Jones, 2005). The analyses of education examined the geographical distribution of speakers of Welsh and identified the importance of areas where high percentages can speak Welsh for the future of the language (Figure 2). Residence in an area where high percentages speak Welsh has previously also been shown to be related to the use an individual makes of the language (Jones, 2008). This chapter will examine out-migration and in particular the relationship between living in a traditionally Welsh-speaking area and out-migration.

The main data source used for this examination is the ONS Longitudinal Study (LS) which is a record linkage study containing census information on a 1 per cent sample of the population of England and Wales.

The same source was used for the previous study of language retention rates (Jones, 2005) which examined the relationship between individuals' ability to speak Welsh in 1991 and 2001. It showed net gains in ability for all age groups identified in the analysis apart from the 65+ age group. One of the issues for further research suggested by the previous analysis was a small refinement to break down the cohort aged 15–24 in the 1991 Census into two: those aged 15–18 who could still be in school and those of post-school age 19–24.

If failing to retain a knowledge of the language from one census to the next can be ruled out, any falls in the *numbers* speaking Welsh must – apart from deaths – be caused by out-migration. (Falls in percentages speaking Welsh can be caused by in-migration). From Figure 1, one can see that numbers reported as able to speak Welsh in 2001 were lower than might have been expected on the basis of the 1991 Census for those aged 18 to 31 in 2001 (and higher for those aged 32 to 56).

For example, the numbers aged 15 in 1991 able to speak Welsh compared to the numbers aged 25 in 2001 showed a 38 per cent drop from 8,462 to 5,262 (Jones, 2005). In percentage terms, they represented respectively 24.6 per cent and 17.4 per cent of their age groups. A similar but smaller drop of 28 per cent was also seen between 1981 and 1991 (Figure 1).

Although there are statistics regarding out-migration from Wales (e.g. National Assembly for Wales, 2005, 2006), few relate to long-term migration, i.e. migration for a period exceeding 12 months (e.g. CeLSIUS, 2007), and fewer deal with the relationship between out-migration and speaking Welsh. One aspect of the latter issue has been examined with a view to estimating the total number of Welsh speakers in the UK (Jones, 2007b) and it gives an indication of the importance of out-migration. It was estimated that 690,000 people could speak Welsh in the UK in 2001, 110,000 of whom were resident in England.

This chapter aims to provide some further evidence regarding:

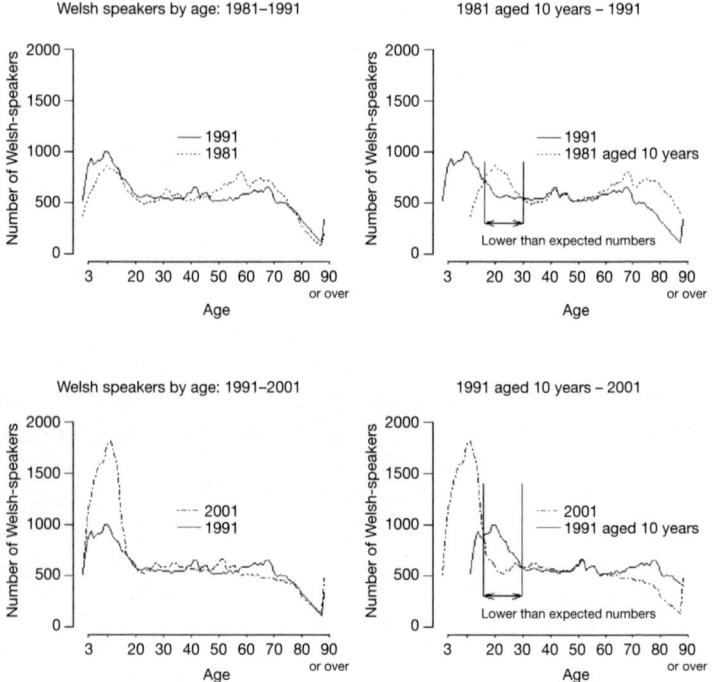

Figure 1

(1) rates of retention of the language amongst people who could speak Welsh when aged 15–24, and
(2) long-term out-migration to England.

Consideration of the latter topic will be in two parts. The first will look at out-migration over 10, 20 and 30 years, distinguishing age groups. The second will look only at out-migration of adults (excluding students) over just ten-year periods and examine the relationship between out-migration to England and various factors including the ability to speak Welsh, area of residence, country of birth, age, sex and social class.

The first section will discuss the methodology used in the analyses. Results will be presented in the second section, followed by discussion of them, and a concluding section.

Methodology

All the analyses were based on the ONS Longitudinal Study. The LS contains details, where available, from the 1971, 1981, 1991 and 2001 Censuses, for members included in the study. The LS is a continuous representative sample of the population of England and Wales only. Subsequent references to percentages moving to England do not actually refer therefore to the whole population emigrating from Wales: migration to elsewhere within the UK or international migration is not considered.

Analysis of the consistency of response to the census presented in Table 1 of the Results section followed the approach used previously (Jones, 2005) with the difference that individuals aged 25–34 in the later census were split into two smaller age groups, 25–8 and 29–34, corresponding roughly to a group likely to contain many still in school ten years earlier (particularly in the more recent censuses) and a group more likely to contain many tertiary-level students. At an all-Wales level, the assumptions made by the Office for National Statistics for their 2006-based population projections make clear that net in-migration to Wales peaks in the 18–19 age group (Office for National Statistics, 2007). In 2000–1, for example, 18,662 Welsh-domiciled undergraduates were enrolled at higher education institutions outside Wales while 25,177 undergraduates domiciled elsewhere in the UK were enrolled at higher education institutions in Wales (HEFCW, 2002). A comparison of numbers able to speak Welsh aged 25–34 in a later census would therefore be including (amongst others) two quite different groups of people in terms of characteristics: those who were school pupils in Wales a decade earlier and still in Wales; and those who were undergraduates in Wales from outside Wales a decade earlier but still in Wales.

The analysis of out-migration to England has two elements. The first step of the analysis – the results of which are presented in Table 5, Table 6 and Table 7 in the following section – was to look at *long-term* out-migration. The ONS LS was simply tabulated to provide data concerning out-migration over 30-, 20- and 10-year periods for:

(1) five different age groups: 3–14, 15–24, 25–34, 35–54 and 55 or over (ages at the time of the earlier census),
(2) for the two sexes separately,

(3) for those with the ability to speak Welsh and those without separately, and

(4) for two separate areas of Wales: a traditionally Welsh-speaking area and the rest of Wales. The traditionally Welsh-speaking area was defined, in terms of the local government geography of 1971, as comprising the districts of Carmarthen, Dinefwr, Llanelli and Ceredigion in the former county of Dyfed, and Anglesey, Arfon, Dwyfor, and Meirionnydd districts in the former county of Gwynedd i.e. roughly the equivalents of the 2001 unitary authorities of Isle of Anglesey, Gwynedd, Ceredigion and Carmarthenshire. These two areas are shown in Figure 2.

The tabulations actually distinguished both out-migration to England and internal migration within Wales, to and fro between the traditionally Welsh-speaking areas and the rest of Wales.

The traditionally Welsh-speaking area, as defined for this analysis, is in the north- and south-west of Wales. No part of the area was contiguous with England and the shortest straight line distance from the point nearest to England was about 20 miles (30 km). For most of

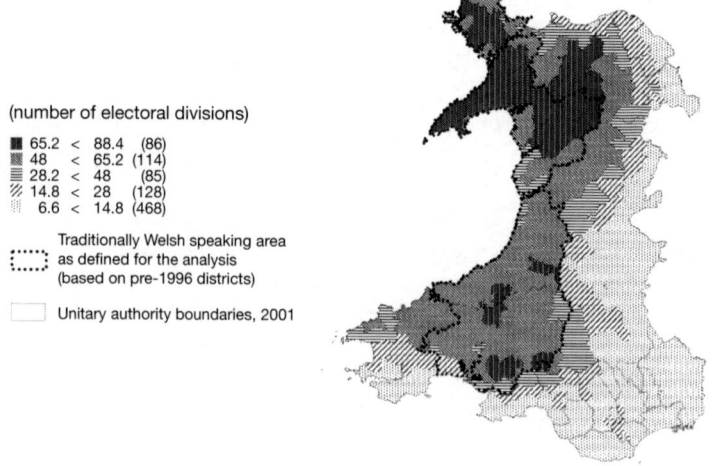

Figure 2 Percentage able to speak Welsh, 2001: all aged 3 and over
Source: 2001 Census. Table CAS146. Crown Copyright 2007. Licence number C02W0002635.

the population the distance by road would be much greater, and the travel time would certainly exceed an hour, particularly in the earlier periods. Most people moving from the traditionally Welsh-speaking area to England could be expected to be moving for job-related reasons. Extremely few would be moving for housing reasons and commuting. Conversely, with the exception of Pembrokeshire in the extreme south-west of Wales, the area defined as the rest of Wales shared the border with England. Some parts of the area, especially in north-east Wales, but also in mid-Wales and south-east Wales, had population concentrations within commuting distance of England. Some of those recorded as migrating from these areas to England could have been moving relatively short distances. Even so, for the bulk of the population in this area, a move to England would have represented a fairly long distance move, probably related to a job move, and could fairly considered be described as a migration. In comparing migration rates to England from the traditionally Welsh-speaking area with migration rates from the rest of Wales we may therefore not be comparing exactly the same phenomenon but we believe the comparison to be a reasonable one to make nevertheless.

High unemployment rates and lower average house prices have been found to be related to high rates of out-migration (Office of the Deputy Prime Minister, 2002). The traditionally Welsh-speaking area lies within the West Wales and the Valleys area which is currently eligible for EU Convergence funding. It is therefore, by definition, a disadvantaged region where GDP per head is less than 75 per cent of the EU average. House prices in the Welsh-speaking area remained low even in 2004 (3 years after the latest data included in the analysis) compared to the GB average although there was considerable variation. The houseprice–to–income ratios through much of the area however were comparatively high (Wilcox, 2005). None of these economic factors have been explicitly included in any of the analyses of this chapter; rather geographic variation between them is subsumed within the simple dichotomous area variable. It needs to be borne in mind that economic factors such as these may be even more important for individuals' decisions concerning migration than their own personal characteristics.

The second element in the analysis of out-migration focussed solely on *adults'* migration over just 10-year periods. As the LS provided data from 1971 to 2001, three separate periods were available for analysis; 1971–81, 1981–91 and 1991–2001. The data for the three periods are not wholly independent of course, as people resident in Wales at a later census will, if still alive at the next census, form part of the LS sample for the next period.

The response variable used in a binomial logistic regression was area of residence (England or Wales) at the time of the later census. The predictor variables used included those listed above but also:

(5) social class at the time of the earlier census, and
(6) country of birth (Wales or outside of Wales).

The social class variable used was the social class variable of 1971, 1981, and 1991 respectively. The variable was very similar in each of those years, being based on occupation.

The analysis excluded some social classes, namely those comprising people whose occupation was inadequately described; those in the armed forces; and students, those of independent means, permanently sick, or housewives. The latter exclusion of students (and children) in particular should be noted. It effectively ensures that the analyses exclude children and is thus an analysis of adults. As the sample only includes those still living at the time of the later census, the sample also excludes those in their last ten years of life at the time of the earlier census.

Given that, as will be seen when the results are discussed, the most mobile section of the population is that of young people, some explanation is due as to why the modelling described here was limited to the migration of adults. There were a number of reasons. First, any age grouping which includes people at different life stages, e.g. in secondary education *and* in tertiary, is potentially omitting a variable of significance which could lead to biased coefficient estimates. As it is known that stage of education is a variable of significance and yet not available for analysis with the LS data set (as it is not collected in the census), excluding that portion of the population where it is likely to be of most significance aimed to limit the problem. Secondly, as neither children nor students are ascribed a social class within the LS, there seemed little utility in including them in an analysis which sought evidence as to the influence of their own social class (as compared to that of their parents) on out-migration. Thirdly, there was the further consideration of the reliability of the coding of place of residence of students. As the treatment of students has varied over the entire period (Brassett-Grundy, 2003), their exclusion seemed advisable.

Table 1 Changes in Welsh-speaking status between two censuses, by age group

Age group at later census and pair of censuses	Per cent changing Welsh-speaking status between censuses		Per cent not changing Welsh-speaking status between censuses		Percent speaking Welsh (in the LS)	
	Could not speak Welsh at earlier census	Could speak Welsh at earlier census	Could not speak Welsh at earlier census	Could speak Welsh at earlier census	at the earlier census	at the later census
25–28						
1971–81	3.9	21.1	96.1	78.9	18.2	17.5
1981–91	3.3	24.3	96.7	75.7	16.5	15.2
1991–2001	3.6	18.4	96.4	81.6	21.7	20.5
29–34						
1971–81	2.5	14.8	97.5	85.2	17.6	17.1
1981–91	2.9	15.0	97.1	85.0	14.9	15.1
1991–2001	5.3	14.1	94.7	85.9	16.1	18.3

Source: ONS Longitudinal Study, author's analysis

The data for each period were modelled separately using individual level data within the safe setting of the ONS Virtual Microdata Laboratory. The initial modelling of tabulated data found some interactions between the ability to speak Welsh and the area of residence and, in 1971–81 and 1991–2001, between Welsh-speaking ability and country of birth. For the presentation of results, modelling was undertaken for Welsh speakers and non-Welsh speakers separately so that the effect of area of residence and country of birth could be identified for each group separately.

The results of the regression analysis are in Table 14 and Table 15 in the following section.

Results

Transition rates

The previous analysis (Jones, 2005) showed that 16 per cent of those aged 15–24 in 1991 who were reported as able to speak Welsh at that time were reported as not being able to speak Welsh in 2001. Conversely, 4.7 per cent of those in the same age group reported as unable to speak Welsh in 1991 were reported as able to speak the language in 2001. The net effect was that a higher percentage (19.1 per cent) of this cohort could speak Welsh in 2001 than in 1991 (18.1 per cent) though these percentages were only significantly different at $p=0.071$ (applying McNemar's test).

Table 1 shows figures for the finer age groups: 25–8 and 29–34 (at the later census) for the three 10-year periods.

For the 25–8 age group, the hypothesis that the odds ratio (odds on speaking Welsh in the later census for those who spoke Welsh in the first: odds on speaking Welsh in the later census for those who did not in the first) was homogeneous over the three decades cannot be rejected (Breslow-Day test, $p=0.719$). For the 29–34 age group however, this null hypothesis of homogeneity of the odds ratio can be rejected with $p=0.051$.

Tests of the marginal homogeneity of the percentages speaking Welsh, i.e. of the significance of differences between the percentages shown in the last two columns of Table 1 showed the only significant difference to be that between 1991 and 2001 for the 29–34 age group (McNemar's, $p=0.001$).

Welsh Speakers: Age Profile and Out-Migration

These are interesting results but perhaps counter-intuitive. Given the growth in the teaching of Welsh as a second language in the wake of the 1988 Education Reform Act, one might have expected an even higher percentage of speakers aged 15–18 in 1991 to have lost their ability by 2001. The opposite seems to have occurred, though the net effect of the transitions was still negative (however, neither of these apparent changes is statistically significant in this sample). Even more encouragingly, in the 19–24 age group the gains are statistically significant.

Returning to the example given in the introduction concerning the 8,462 15-year-olds able to speak Welsh in 1991, using the transition rates presented above for the 15–18 age group it can be calculated that in 2001 one might have expected 7,836 of the cohort to be able to speak Welsh, a fall of around 7 per cent. Instead, the 2001 Census reported 5,262 *in Wales,* a figure 33 per cent lower than that expected. Similarly, applying transition rates to the 1981 figures, one might have expected a fall of 8 per cent, giving 7,222 25-year-olds able to speak Welsh in 1991. The 5,638 reported in Wales in 1991 is 22 per cent lower than that. These discrepancies, of 33 per cent between 1991 and 2001, and 22 per cent between 1981 and 1991, can be considered as estimates of the percentages of Welsh-speakers migrating from Wales, based on census numbers, modified by estimates of language transition rates derived from the ONS Longitudinal Study. But the Longitudinal Study can itself provide direct estimates of rates of out-migration to England.

Table 2 shows the percentage of 15-year-old Welsh speakers who migrated to England in 1971–81, 1981–91, and 1991–2001. The confidence intervals for 1981–91 and 1991–2001 both include the

Table 2 15-year-old Welsh speakers: out-migration to England in 1971–81, 1981–91, 1991–2001

	15-year-old Welsh-speakers in sample	*% of 15-year-old Welsh-speakers migrating from Wales to England*	
		Point estimate	*95% Confidence interval*
1971–81	66	7.6	3.3–16.5
1981–91	72	18.1	10.9–28.5
1991–01	83	37.3	27.7–48.1

Source: ONS Longitudinal Study, author's analysis

Table 3 Percentage of the population born in Wales, 1971 to 2001

	Dyfed	Gwynedd	Wales
1971	87.0	73.4	81.2
1981	79.8	70.9	79.5
1991	74.6	67.4	77.2
2001	n.a.	n.a.	75.4

Source: National Assembly for Wales, 1998: Table 1.8 and 2001 Census.

percentage drops shown in the previous paragraph so these results can be considered as consistent with those derived in the previous paragraph. Around a third of 1991's 15-year-old Welsh speakers had migrated to England by 2001. Rates of migration to England are considered again later but using broader age bands.

The traditionally Welsh-speaking area and in-migration

As the subsequent analyses will compare the traditionally Welsh-speaking area's experience of out-migration with the rest of Wales, and a link between in- and out-migration will be identified, a brief review of the in-migration to this area is in order.

In every year from 1981 to 2001, Wales experienced positive net in-migration from the rest of the UK (Welsh Assembly Government, 2007). The traditionally Welsh-speaking area, much of which is attractive country and seaside, was the focus of much of it. The 1970s too had seen in-migration to Dyfed and Gwynedd, the counties which contain the traditionally Welsh-speaking areas. In-migration was less common before that. Of the traditionally Welsh-speaking area only Anglesey, Caernarvonshire, and Cardiganshire experienced net in-migration between 1961 and 1971: Merionethshire and Carmarthenshire experienced net out-migration. Table 3 shows the resultant trend in the percentage of the population born in Wales.

As well as in-migration reflecting the general urban–rural drift, specific influences will have an effect. It needs to be borne in mind that the traditionally Welsh-speaking area contained colleges of the University of Wales in Aberystwyth, Bangor and Lampeter. Those in Aberystwyth and Bangor in particular underwent a considerable expansion in the 1971–2001 period. Although for this chapter individuals classed as students were excluded from the regression analyses which will be reported, university staff would be included and many would be counted amongst the professional occupations. Similarly, a number of major hospitals were, and are, to be found in the traditionally Welsh-speaking area. These include Ysbyty Gwynedd in Bangor, Ysbyty Glangwili in Carmarthen, Prince Philip Hospital in Llanelli and Ysbyty Bronglais in Aberystwyth. Many of their staff would again be counted among the professional and managerial occupations and many, probably the vast majority, in those occupations would be in-migrants. It is the significance of those latter sectors and the paucity of other opportunities within the traditionally Welsh-speaking area which are likely to be the cause too of the high out-migration rates seen among the non-Welsh speakers with professional and managerial occupations. The relatively low percentages of Welsh speakers amongst managers and senior officials (Table 4) lend support to the existence of spiralism. (For discussion of spiralism and the distribution of Welsh and non-Welsh speakers in the 1981 and 1991 Censuses, by social class, occupation and geography, see Williams and Morris, 2000, and by gender, Jones and Morris, 1997).

The various forms of local government represent another major source of employment within the traditionally Welsh-speaking area, although in that sector locally born staff are likely to form a much

Table 4 Percentage able to speak Welsh in the traditionally Welsh speaking area; the economically active; in the industries of public administration etc. and health and social work; amongst managers, senior officials and professionals, by county

		Percentage able to speak Welsh			
		By industry (SIC92)		By occupation (SOC2000)	
	Total economically active	Public administration and defence; social security	Health and social work	Managers and senior officials	Professional
Isle of Anglesey	59.2	51.2[†]	63.4	44.4	60.7
Gwynedd	69.2	78.0	70.8	54.4	68.4
Ceredigion	51.8	57.9	47.4	43.2	53.4
Carmarthenshire	46.4	49.9	45.1	39.9	53.0

†: The Isle of Anglesey has an RAF airbase at Valley.
Source: 2001 Census theme table T39

larger proportion of the staff than in the higher education and health sectors, again as suggested by the figures in Table 4.

Though 9 per cent of the population of Wales aged 3 and over born outside Wales could speak Welsh in 2001, adults were less integrated linguistically. For example, only 5.0 per cent of the population of Wales aged 45–64 born outside Wales could speak Welsh. In the four authorities of the traditionally Welsh-speaking area this percentage varied from 12.4 per cent in the Isle of Anglesey and 16.7 per cent in Gwynedd to 11.9 per cent in Ceredigion and 9.5 per cent in Carmarthenshire (2001 Census, theme table T39) (Hartwell et al., 2007:37, reports 9.9 per cent of recent immigrants to 'rural Wales' as fluent Welsh speakers).

Out-migration: people of all ages

Tables 5 to 7 give some quantification to the extent of out-migration over 30-, 20- and 10-year periods. Looking at those who were children aged 3 to 14 in 1971, Table 5 shows that thirty years later, of those still resident in England or Wales, nearly one-fifth of them (19.4 per cent) were living in England. Table 6 shows how rates differed for Welsh speakers and non-Welsh speakers across the whole of Wales, while Table 7 provides the same comparison in respect of people living in the traditionally Welsh-speaking area. From the traditionally Welsh-speaking area in particular, the percentages of non-Welsh speakers moving to England were generally much higher than the percentages

Table 5 Percentage moving to England over 30, 20 and 10-year periods: all people, by age group, by sex

	% moving to England								
	All			Males			Females		
Age in earlier census	1971–2001	1981–2001	1991–2001	1971–2001	1981–2001	1991–2001	1971–2001	1981–2001	1991–2001
3–14	19.4	20.7	11.2	20.4	21.2	11.6	18.4	20.3	10.8
15–24	14.7	15.5	16.8	15.4	16.7	17.8	14.1	14.3	16.0
25–34	9.3	9.1	8.7	9.9	10.2	10.2	8.8	8.1	7.3
35–54	5.4	4.8	4.0	5.7	5.7	4.5	5.2	3.9	3.5
55+	8.2	6.3	4.0	9.0	5.8	3.9	7.9	6.5	4.0

Source: ONS Longitudinal Study, author's analysis.

Table 6 Percentage moving to England over 30-, 20- and 10-year periods: Welsh speakers and non-Welsh speakers, by age group

	% moving to England					
	Welsh speakers			Non-Welsh speakers		
Age in earlier census	1971–2001	1981–2001	1991–2001	1971–2001	1981–2001	1991–2001
3–14	16.8	17.7	12.1	19.9	21.4	10.9
15–24	11.7	13.1	15.0	15.4	15.9	17.2
25–34	2.9	6.3	2.8	10.6	9.6	9.6
35–54	1.5	1.1	1.9	6.5	5.6	4.4
55+	1.4	1.3	1.2	11.0	7.9	4.7

Source: ONS Longitudinal Study, author's analysis.

Table 7 Percentage moving from traditionally Welsh speaking areas to England over 30-, 20- and 10-year periods: by language, by age group

	% moving to England								
	All people			Welsh speakers			Non-Welsh speakers		
Age in earlier census	1971–2001	1981–2001	1991–2001	1971–2001	1981–2001	1991–2001	1971–2001	1981–2001	1991–2001
3–14	20.3	22.2	13.1	15.5	16.2	12.0	28.9	33.9	15.8
15–24	15.3	16.4	21.4	11.8	12.7	15.6	24.1	21.1	31.9
25–34	9.4	7.5	10.1	3.0	4.0	0.8	21.4	12.4	21.0
35–54	3.5	4.3	5.9	0.5	0.9	2.4	10.7	9.8	10.5
55+	2.3	4.6	4.8	0.0	0.8	0.8	10.5	12.7	10.9

Source: ONS Longitudinal Study, author's analysis.

of Welsh speakers moving. This finding was the stimulus for the subsequent examination of the significance of language, age, sex and area of residence in the out-migration of adults. It will be seen later that another factor – country of birth – not included in the tables shown in this section, is found to be important. Note that from Table 5 and Table 7 one can gather that over 1991–2001, and over the 20- and 30-year-periods, higher percentages of people aged under 25 moved to England from the traditionally Welsh-speaking area than from the rest of Wales.

Table 8 The composition of the matched LS survey sample by social class*

		Number in earlier census			Percent in earlier census		
Social class		1971–81	1981–91	1991–2001	1971–81	1981–91	1991–2001
I	Professional Occupations	331	389	485	3.1	3.3	3.5
II	Managerial and Technical Occupations	2,098	2,555	3,432	19.5	21.4	24.5
IIIN	Skilled Non-manual Occupations	1,961	2,452	3,188	18.2	20.5	22.7
IIIM	Skilled Manual Occupations	3,245	3,216	3,170	30.2	27.0	22.6
IV	Partly-Skilled Occupations	2,200	2,349	2,653	20.4	19.7	18.9
V	Unskilled Occupations	925	972	1,087	8.6	8.1	7.8
Total		10,760	11,933	14,015	100.0	100.0	100.0

* Excluding those comprising people whose occupation was inadequately described; those in the armed forces; and students, those of independent means, permanently sick, or housewives.
Source: ONS Longitudinal Study, author's analysis.

Out-migration: 'adults' excluding students

We turn now to the regression analyses of out-migration of one segment of the population, roughly described as 'adults' excluding students. The effective numbers included in this analysis which was limited to those resident in Wales in the earlier year and either Wales

Table 9 Percentage* speaking Welsh, by area of residence in Wales at the earlier census

	% Welsh-speaking in the earlier census		
Area of residence in the earlier census	1971–81	1981–91	1991–2001
Rest of Wales	13.5	11.9	9.2
Traditionally Welsh-speaking area	72.0	60.5	58.4
Wales total	21.5	18.4	16.1

* Excluding people whose occupation was inadequately described; those in the armed forces; and students, those of independent means, permanently sick, or housewives
Source: ONS Longitudinal Study, author's analysis

Table 10 Effect of not speaking Welsh on odds of out-migration to England

Period	Odds ratio (multiplicative effect on out-migration of not speaking Welsh compared to speaking Welsh)	Significance
1971–81	1.37	0.053
1981–91	1.80	<0.001
1991–2001	1.94	<0.001

Source: ONS Longitudinal Study, author's analysis

or England in the latter year with complete data for the variables included, were 10,760 for 1971–81, 11,933 in 1981–91 and 14,015 in 1991–2001. The distribution of the sample shows a drift from 1971 to 1991 from Social Class III, Skilled Manual Occupations to the higher classes.[1]

Table 9 shows how the percentage speaking Welsh amongst the matched LS sample members fell from 21.5 per cent in 1971 to 16.1 per cent in 1991. Although in percentage terms the traditionally Welsh-speaking area recorded a smaller fall than did the rest of Wales – falling 19 per cent (–13.6 percentage points) from 72 per cent to 58.4 per cent, compared to a fall of –32 per cent (–4.3 percentage points) from 13.5 per cent to 9.2 per cent – that means that Welsh was far less prevalent in the area by the 1990s.

Table 11 tabulates rates of out-migration for various subgroups separately. The rates by age group for 1991–2001 can be compared with those in Table 5, bearing in mind that they are based on different populations. Note that the percentage migrating to England from the traditionally Welsh-speaking area was higher than that from the rest of Wales only over 1991–2001. Higher percentages of the Professional social class emigrated than from any other class, higher percentages of non-Welsh-speakers than Welsh speakers emigrated, higher percentages of those born outside Wales emigrated than of those born in Wales, and generally the younger age groups had higher percentages moving to England than the older age groups.

From Table 12, one can see that the rate of migration to England of those born outside Wales is at least three times that of those born in Wales, whether one considers Welsh speakers or non-Welsh-speakers.

Table 13's figures suggest that the rate of migration to England of those born outside Wales varies little between those living in the traditionally Welsh-speaking area and those living elsewhere in Wales. For those born in Wales, rates of migration to England in the decades 1971–81 and 1981–91 were lower from the traditionally Welsh-speaking area than from the rest of Wales but the situation changed in the period 1991–2001.

Before proceeding to report the results of the separate logistic regressions for Welsh and non-Welsh speakers, the results of applying the same model to the combined sample, without terms for interactions with area but including an additional variable for speaking Welsh, are shown in Table 10. Not speaking Welsh increased the odds of out-migration by 37 per cent in 1971–81 but by 94 per cent in 1991–2001.

Table 14 and Table 15 present the results of attempting to fit the logistic model to the Welsh-speakers and non-Welsh speakers separately.

Being aged 15–24 had the biggest effect on the odds of out-migration for Welsh speakers, exceeding the effect of country of birth in each period. For non-Welsh speakers being aged 25–34 was also a significant factor in each period, although with less of an effect on the odds than country of birth. For non-Welsh speakers country of birth had a bigger effect on the odds of out-migration in 1971–81 and 1981–91 than did being aged 15–24. By 1991–2001 however, the effect of being aged 15–24 was for non-Welsh speakers larger than that of country of birth, as it was for Welsh speakers.

After age, the factor with the generally largest significant effects was country of birth. For a non-Welsh-speaker, being born outside Wales increases the odds of out-migration at least threefold (365 per cent in 1981–91). The significance of effects for those born outside Wales but who could speak Welsh was lower in 1971–81 and 1991–2001. In those periods, the size of the effects was lower than for non-Welsh speakers, i.e. for those born outside Wales but who could speak Welsh, the odds on out-migration was lower than for those who could not speak Welsh. If one accepts that being able to speak Welsh is an indication of a degree of integration, this is what one might have expected: being able to speak Welsh is associated with subsequently staying in Wales rather than moving out. However, the picture is not clear-cut, as in 1981–91 the odds ratio for those born outside Wales but able to speak Welsh was highly significant and large – increasing the odds on out-migration nearly sevenfold (677 per cent) – larger than any of the effects of being born outside Wales for non-Welsh speakers.

Table 11 Percentage moving to England, by single category in the earlier census

	% who moved to England		
	1971–81	1981–91	1991–2001
From area of residence in earlier census			
Rest of Wales	5.5	5.7	6.2
Traditionally Welsh-speaking area	4.3	5.3	7.8
Social class at earlier census			
I Professional	14.7	17.3	11.3
II Intermediate	8.6	7.4	7.9
IIIN Skilled non-manual	7.2	6.7	7.0
IIIM Skilled manual	3.3	4.0	4.3
IV Partly Skilled	3.5	4.0	6.8
V Unskilled	2.6	3.0	3.5
Welsh-speaking category at earlier census			
Welsh-speaking	2.5	2.3	3.0
Non-Welsh-speaking	6.0	6.2	7.1
Country of birth			
Outside Wales	15.6	14.5	16.5
Wales	3.1	3.2	3.1
Sex			
Male	5.0	5.7	6.5
Female	6.2	5.6	6.3
Age			
15–24	9.3	10.1	13.5
25–34	7.3	7.5	8.6
35–54	3.4	4.0	3.9
55+	3.5	3.1	3.3
Total	5.4	5.7	6.4
Number	*581*	*679*	*903*

Note: Table based on all for whom area of residence in the later census was recorded. Excluding those comprising people whose occupation was inadequately described; those in the armed forces; and students, those of independent means, permanently sick, or housewives.
Source: ONS Longitudinal Study, author's analysis.

Table 12 Percentage moving to England, by country of birth by Welsh-speaking category at the earlier census

		% who moved to England		
		1971–81	1981–91	1991–2001
Welsh-speaking category at earlier census	Country of birth			
Welsh-speaking				
	Outside Wales	8.5	12.7	7.8
	Wales	2.3	1.6	2.6
	Total	2.5	2.3	3.0
Non-Welsh-speaking				
	Outside Wales	15.6	14.1	17.0
	Wales	3.2	3.5	3.2
	Total	6.0	6.2	7.1

Note: Excluding people whose occupation was inadequately described; those in the armed forces; and students, those of independent means, permanently sick, or housewives.
Source: ONS Longitudinal Study, author's analysis.

Area of residence had a highly significant effect for non-Welsh speakers only in the most recent period, i.e. in 1991–2001. Living in the traditionally Welsh-speaking area then increased the odds on out-migration by 69 per cent. For Welsh speakers, area of residence was significant only in 1981–91: living in the traditionally Welsh-speaking area then reduced the odds of out-migration for them by around half.

For Welsh speakers social class had some significance for out-migration in the earlier periods but even then it was limited. For non-Welsh speakers, social class was significant in each period. Generally, odds on out-migrating were significantly lower for most social classes compared with the odds on out-migration for those in the professional class for all periods, although by the 1991–2001 period only two classes had significantly lower odds.

Sex was generally not a significant factor. Only for non-Welsh speakers in the 1991–2001 period did males appear to have significantly higher odds of migration to England than females.

Table 13 Percentage moving to England, by country of birth by area of residence at the earlier census

		% who moved to England		
		1971–81	1981–91	1991–2001
Country of birth	Area of residence in earlier census			
Outside Wales				
	Rest of Wales	15.3	13.7	15.9
	Traditionally Welsh-speaking area	15.3	15.7	19.1
	Total	15.3	14.0	16.5
Wales				
	Rest of Wales	3.2	3.3	3.1
	Traditionally Welsh-speaking area	1.8	1.6	3.3
	Total	3.0	3.1	3.1

Note: Excluding people whose occupation was inadequately described; those in the armed forces; and students, those of independent means, permanently sick, or housewives.
Source: ONS Longitudinal Study, author's analysis.

Discussion

The results presented concerning retention and out-migration rates clearly indicate that the lower than expected numbers of young adult Welsh speakers in the 2001 Census were a consequence of out-migration, not of a failure by individuals to retain their Welsh-speaking ability. The following discussion concentrates on the issue of migration therefore.

Data concerning in-migration were presented before proceeding to the analysis of out-migration as an association between past movement and current mobility is commonly found. Family-related issues and, recently, friendship networks and social ties have been shown to play a major role in mobility decisions (Donovan et al., 2002; Belot and Ermisch, 2006). Previous increases in in-migration can be expected, as social ties etc. are weakened, to lead to subsequent increases of out-migration.

Table 14 Results of logistic regression for Welsh speakers

	1971–81			1981–91			1991–2001		
	Sig	Odds ratio	95% confidence interval	Sig	Odds ratio	95% confidence interval	Sig	Odds ratio	95% confidence interval
Area (reference group = Rest of Wales other than traditionally Welsh-speaking area)									
	n.s.	0.60	(0.35, 1.07)	*	0.53	(0.28, 0.99)	n.s.	1.08	(0.66, 1.77)
Social class (reference group = I Professional Occupations)									
	**			n.s.			n.s.		
II Intermediate	n.s.	0.41	(0.14, 1.22)	*	0.31	(0.10, 0.97)	n.s.	0.60	(0.19, 1.86)
IIIN Skilled non-manual	n.s.	0.61	(0.20, 1.86)	n.s.	0.49	(0.15, 1.59)	n.s.	0.40	(0.12, 1.33)
IIIM Skilled manual	***	**0.08**	(0.02, 0.31)	*	**0.25**	(0.08, 0.84)	n.s.	0.65	(0.21, 2.06)
IV Partly Skilled	*	**0.23**	(0.07, 0.78)	n.s.	0.41	(0.12, 1.35)	n.s.	0.42	(0.12, 1.43)
V Unskilled	n.s.	0.33	(0.08, 1.33)	n.s.	0.27	(0.05, 1.50)	n.s.	0.67	(0.17, 2.69)

	Model 1			Model 2			Model 3		
	Sig	OR	(95% CI)	Sig	OR	(95% CI)	Sig	OR	(95% CI)
Country of birth (reference group = Wales)	**	3.53	(1.47, 8.44)	***	7.77	(3.99, 15.1)	**	2.84	(1.54, 5.25)
Sex (reference group = Females)	n.s.	1.13	(0.63, 2.03)	n.s.	0.93	(0.49, 1.78)	n.s.	0.89	(0.52, 1.52)
Age (reference group = 55 and over)	***			***			***		
15–24	***	**5.60**	(2.41, 13.02)	***	**8.42**	(3.05, 23.2)	***	**8.00**	(3.22, 19.83)
25–34	n.s.	2.35	(0.95, 5.82)	**	**4.57**	(1.63, 12.80)	n.s.	2.51	(0.95, 6.63)
35–54	n.s.	0.96	(0.39, 2.35)	n.s.	0.85	(0.26, 2.74)	n.s.	1.88	(0.75, 4.71)
Constant	***	**0.03**		***	**0.02**		***	**0.02**	
Model fit									
$X^2 =$		67.3, 11 df			89.9, 11 df			46.2, 11 df	
Nagelkerke's $R^2=$		0.137			0.203			0.085	
N=		2,318			2,200			2,266	

Notes: Excluding people whose occupation was inadequately described; those in the armed forces; and students, those of independent means, permanently sick, or housewives.
Significance (Sig) of variables marked: *** <=0.001; ** <=0.01; * <=0.05; n.s. not significant.
Odds ratios of variables with significance levels <=0.05 are in bold.
Source: ONS Longitudinal Study, author's analysis.

Table 15 Results of logistic regression for non-Welsh-speakers

	1971–81			1981–91			1991–2001		
	Sig	Odds ratio	95% confidence interval	Sig	Odds ratio	95% confidence interval	Sig	Odds ratio	95% confidence interval
Area (reference group = Rest of Wales other than traditionally Welsh-speaking area)									
	n.s.	1.00	(0.69, 1.45)	n.s.	1.16	(0.87, 1.55)	***	**1.69**	(1.35, 2.13)
Social class (reference group = I Professional Occupations)	***			***			***		
II Intermediate	n.s.	0.73	(0.49, 1.09)	***	**0.47**	(0.33, 0.67)	n.s.	0.89	(0.63, 1.26)
IIIN Skilled non-manual	***	**0.47**	(0.30, 0.71)	***	**0.37**	(0.25, 0.53)	n.s.	0.70	(0.48, 1.01)
IIIM Skilled manual	***	**0.28**	(0.19, 0.42)	***	**0.23**	(0.16, 0.33)	***	**0.38**	(0.26, 0.56)
IV Partly Skilled	***	**0.25**	(0.16, 0.39)	***	**0.25**	(0.17, 0.37)	n.s.	0.73	(0.51, 1.05)
V Unskilled	***	**0.21**	(0.12, 0.38)	***	**0.20**	(0.12, 0.33)	***	**0.37**	(0.23, 0.60)

	Sig	Value	CI	Sig	Value	CI	Sig	Value	CI
Country of birth (reference group = Wales)	***	**5.77**	(4.74, 7.03)	***	**4.65**	(3.89, 5.56)	***	**7.11**	(6.04, 8.37)
Sex (reference group = Females)	n.s.	0.89	(0.71, 1.11)	n.s.	1.15	(0.95, 1.41)	*	1.22	(1.03, 1.43)
Age (reference group = 55 and over)	***			***			***		
15–24	***	**3.55**	(2.59, 4.89)	***	**4.51**	(3.35, 6.07)	***	**7.82**	(5.93, 10.31)
25–34	***	**2.44**	(1.77, 3.37)	***	**2.43**	(1.81, 3.26)	***	**3.45**	(2.65, 4.50)
35–54	n.s.	1.03	(0.75, 1.41)	n.s.	1.26	(0.94, 1.68)	n.s.	1.20	(0.92, 1.58)
Constant	***	**0.05**		***	**0.05**		***	**0.02**	
Model fit									
$X^2 =$		542.7, 11 df			533.5, 11 df			1056.8, 11 df	
Nagelkerke's $R^2 =$		0.171			0.144			0.215	
N =		8,441			9,733			11,749	

Source: ONS Longitudinal Study, author's analysis.
Notes: see Table 14.

One consequence of the long-term in-migration will have been to the social capital within the area (Donovan et al., 2002; Putnam, 2007). Family and other social networks will have become less locally focused. (For one linguistic consequence of this, see Centre for European Research (Wales) and Cwmni Iaith, 2006.)

The results of the 2001 Census (Table 4) are indicative of the existence of spiralism in the labour market whereby workers are geographically and socially mobile, i.e. moving from one area to another to progress their careers. The results of the regression analyses presented (Table 14 and Table 15) are further evidence of this spiralism. For the last thirty years they showed that age was generally the most significant factor associated with out-migration, but being born outside Wales generally had an effect of similar magnitude as being aged 15–24, particularly for non-Welsh speakers. Whereas social class had little effect amongst Welsh speakers, it was highly significant for non-Welsh speakers, though distinctions between the professional class and the intermediate and skilled non-manual classes faded by 1991–2001 even for non-Welsh speakers.

Individuals in the professional social class will be highly qualified so that references to being of professional class can be interpreted also as being highly qualified, i.e. a reference to human capital. Other work on migration from Wales (over one year) has similarly shown that the propensity to out-migrate is greater for individuals with high qualifications (Drinkwater and Blackaby, 2004).

It is known that mobility, i.e. the percentage moving house, varies by age with single young adults forming the largest proportion of moving within a year (Bailey and Livingston, 2005; Donovan et al., 2002). Although out-migration refers to a longer-term phenomenon, the finding of a relationship between out-migration and youth was still to be expected.

One stimulus for this analysis is the importance of the traditionally Welsh-speaking area for the future of the Welsh language. Low rates of linguistic integration of people born outside Wales are the major reason why the percentage able to speak Welsh in the traditionally Welsh-speaking area has been falling (Table 3 and Table 9). The regression analyses suggest that in spite of their lack of linguistic integration, residence in a traditionally Welsh-speaking area was not associated with higher odds on out-migration of adult non-Welsh speakers until the 1991–2001 period. The analysis cannot provide a reason for that apparent change but it could be a reflection of a change in labour market or other conditions peculiar to the area.

The result that in the 1991–2001 period, the lack of ability to speak Welsh when resident in a traditionally Welsh-speaking area was significantly associated with out-migration may be an indication of relatively weak social ties. A recent small-scale sociological investigation provides some examples of in-migrants' experiences which lend support to this (Day et al., 2006). One obvious policy implication arising from this would be that the teaching of Welsh to adults should be intensified in an attempt to build social capital in order to retain the human capital of the otherwise highly qualified individuals in the traditionally Welsh-speaking area.

As the regression analyses will not have included any people in their last ten years of life at the time of the earlier census one specific trend which probably is to be found in the traditionally Welsh-speaking area has not been examined. This is the phenomenon of return migration of older people, i.e. those aged 75 or over, with long-term limiting illness. In the view of Raymer et al., 2007, this is best represented by migration from coastal and countryside to centres with industry. The NS 2001 Area Classification for Local Authorities (Office for National Statistics, 2005) classifies the four local authorities included in the definition of the traditionally Welsh-speaking area to the Coastal and Countryside cluster so it is to be expected that return migration of older people is a feature of the traditionally Welsh-speaking area.

Despite the time spent in this paper discussing out-migration of adults, the percentages of children emigrating are far higher and arguably of much more importance for the sustainability of a Welsh-speaking population in Wales. Most will recognize the inevitability that many young people will wish to move away from home as they grow up, and that urban centres will be especially attractive because of the recreational and career opportunities they offer (e.g. Jones and Young, 2003, quoted in Dafis, 2004). Initiatives such as the Welsh Assembly government's Llwybro-Routes project whose mission is 'The promotion of staying in rural Wales or returning to rural Wales as attractive and viable options' (Welsh Assembly Government, 2008a) are already directed at the issue. One rationale for such initiatives from the point of view of concern for the revitalization of Welsh is that it makes sense to attempt to minimize leakage from the system in the form of out-migration from Wales so that the return on investment in human capital – specifically teaching Welsh in the education system – should be maximized. According to the 2001 Census, 16,241 (42.8 per cent) of 15-year-olds in Wales were able to speak Welsh compared with 5,262 (17.4 per cent) of 25-year-olds. As noted previously, that number of 25-year-olds was 33 per cent lower than might have been expected on the basis of those speaking Welsh a decade earlier, and it seems as if out-migration, rather than loss of knowledge of the language, could account for that drop. Aiming to reduce the level of out-migration makes sense from the point of view of maximizing the benefit of the education system to the language-regeneration effort.

One other feature should be discussed, namely the general non-significance of social class on the odds of migration to England of Welsh speakers. In terms of those factors associated with migration already considered, one might conjecture that social capital – familial ties especially – might be part of an explanation. One might also conjecture that the development of Wales as a political entity, increasingly from the 1980s, with the related development of job opportunities especially in the public sector in south-east Wales, may also form part of the explanation. Are the bright lights of Cardiff and its environs drawing Welsh speakers of all classes? There is some evidence that they are. An analysis of moves in the year preceding the 2001 Census shows that of people with Welsh-language skills living in the traditionally Welsh-speaking area who moved outside their local authority, 15 per cent moved to Cardiff. The comparable percentage for those with no skills in Welsh was 10 per cent (author's unpublished analysis of Census SMS tables MG101 and MG110).

Conclusion

Most official statistics concerning migration to and from Wales (e.g. Welsh Assembly Government, 2007 and 2008b) concentrate on annual flows, and the cumulative effects, other than in terms of net migration, are not apparent, nor calculable from the published figures. The analyses reported in the chapter add to the knowledge base by providing some indication of the cumulative impact of in- and out-migration over several decades.

The lower than expected numbers of young adult Welsh speakers in the 2001 Census appears to be a consequence of out-migration, not of a failure by individuals to retain their Welsh-speaking ability.

By 2001, one in five of Wales's children of 1971 had moved to England. Not unexpectedly, all the analyses presented suggest that the percentage of the population out-migrating has increased over the period since 1971. While, for adults, it has been shown that the ability to speak Welsh is related to the likelihood of out-migrating, whether one was born in Wales or outside the country has been shown to have a greater effect. Even if those born outside Wales learn to speak Welsh, they are still more likely to move out.

Being able to speak Welsh, whether born in Wales or outside Wales, is associated with lower odds on out-migration. Teaching Welsh to in-migrants may increase their local social ties and social capital, and as a result lower the odds on their out-migrating subsequently.

The extent of out-migration of Welsh speakers from Wales will clearly continue to be an important factor in the success of the language-revitalization effort.

Acknowledgements

ONS LS project number 20080 (clearance number 20080D) provided the basis for this chapter.

Notes

[1] The distribution of the 1991 sample compares reasonably to that shown for the restricted category of residents aged 16 and over, employees and self-employed shown in a published tabulation of 10 per cent of the 1991 Census population: Table 93, 1991 Census Report for Wales (Part 2).

References

Bailey, N. and Livingston, M. (2005). 'Determinants of individual migration: an analysis of SARs data', SCRSJ Working Paper No. 3, Glasgow, Scottish Centre for Research on Social Justice. University of Glasgow.

Belot, M. and Ermisch, J. (2006). 'Friendship ties and geographical mobility: evidence from the BHPS', ISER Working Paper 2006–33, Colchester, Institute for Social and Economic Research.

Blackaby, D. and Drinkwater, S. (1997). 'Welsh speakers and the labour market', *Contemporary Wales*, 9, 158–70.

Brassett-Grundy, A. (2003). LS User Guide 20, *Researching Households and Families Using the ONS Longitudinal Study*, London, Office for National Statistics.

CeLSIUS (2007). Downloadable tables from the ONS Longitudinal Study, *http://www.celsius.lshtm.ac.uk/download/wt090300.html*
Centre for European Research (Wales) and Cwmni Iaith (2006). *Young People's Social Networks and Language Use: Final Report*, Cardiff, Welsh Language Board.
Champion, A. (2007). 'Allowing for the effect of migration in calculating future needs of affordable housing in rural areas', presentation to the 2007 conference of the British Society for Population Studies, *http://www.lse.ac.uk/collections/BSPS/ppt/2007_migration_Champion2.ppt*
Dafis, C. (2004). 'Migration, identity and development', *Agenda* (Summer 2004), Cardiff, Institute of Welsh Affairs.
Day, G., Davis, H. and Drakakis-Smith, A. (2006). 'Being English in north Wales: inmigration and the inmigrant experience', *Nationalism and Ethnic Politics*, 12, 3, 577–98.
Donovan, N., Pilch, T. and Rubenstein, T. (2002). *Geographic Mobility*, London, Performance and Innovation Unit, Cabinet Office.
Drinkwater, S. and Blackaby, D. (2004). 'Migration and labour market differences: the case of Wales', IZA Discussion Paper No. 1275, available at SSRN: *http://ssrn.com/abstract=585309*
Hartwell, S., Kitchen, L., Milbourne, P. and Morgan, S. (2007). 'Population change in rural Wales', Social and Cultural Impacts Research Report No. 14, Wales Rural Observatory, accessed on 6 June 2008, *http://www.walesruralobservatory.org.uk/reports/english/MigrationReport_Final.pdf*
Higher Education Funding Council for Wales (HEFCW) and National Council for Education and Learning Wales (NC-ELWa) (2002). 'Higher education, further education and training statistics in Wales: 2000/01', accessed 6 June 2008, *http://www.elwa.org.uk/ElwaWeb/elwa.aspx?pageid=1867*
Huws, M. (2007). 'Her y Mewnlifiad', *Barn*, 26–7 (April).
Jones, H. (2005). 'Ability to speak Welsh in the Censuses of Population: a longitudinal analysis', *Population Trends*, 122 (Winter 2005), London, Office for National Statistics (Palgrave Macmillan).
—— (2007a). 'Goblygiadau newidiadau ym mhroffil oedran siaradwyr Cymraeg a'u dosbarthiad gofodol', *Gwerddon*, I, 2 (Autumn), 10–37, *www.gwerddon.org*
—— (2007b). 'Estimation of the number of Welsh speakers in England', Welsh Language Board, accessed on 6 June 2008, *www.byig-wlb.org.uk*
—— (2008). 'The changing social context of Welsh: a review of statistical trends', *International Journal of Bilingual Education and Bilingualism*, 11, 5 (September), 541–57.
Jones, G. W. and Young, E. (2003). *A Bright Future for Rural Wales*, Bangor, Centre for Enterprise and Regional Development, University of Wales.
Jones, K. and Morris, D. (1997). *Gender and the Welsh Language: A Research Review*, Cardiff, Equal Opportunities Commission.
Moseley, M. J. and Pahl, R. E. (2007). 'Social capital in rural places', a report to Defra, Rural Evidence Research Centre, accessed on 6 June 2008, *http://www.rerc.ac.uk/*

National Assembly for Wales (1998). *Digest of Welsh Historical Statistics 1974–1996*, Cardiff, National Assembly for Wales.

—— (2005). 'Patterns of migration for Wales: rest of the UK and international', Statistical Bulletin 50/2005, *http://new.wales.gov.uk/topics/statistics/*

—— (2006). 'Patterns of migration in Wales', Statistical Bulletin 10/2006, *http://new.wales.gov.uk/topics/statistics/*

Office of the Deputy Prime Minister (2002). 'Migration model publication summary: Housing Research Summary No. 167, London, ODPM.

Office for National Statistics (2005). 'National statistics area classification', *http://www.statistics.gov.uk/about/methodology_by_theme/area_classification/default.asp*

—— (2007). 'Assumed net migration for 2006-based population projections (principal type)', accessed on 6 May 2008, *http://www.gad.gov.uk/Demography_Data/Population/*

—— (2007). 'Internal migration 2005–2006 local authority flows by quinary age group and gender', accessed on 6 May 2008, *http://www.statistics.gov.uk/statbase/Expodata/Spreadsheets/D9676.xls*

Putnam, R. D. (2007). '*E pluribus unum*: diversity and community in the twenty-first century', *Scandinavian Political Studies*, 30, 2.

Raymer, J., Abel, G. and Smith, P.W.F. (2007). 'Combining census and registration data to estimate detailed elderly migration flows in England and Wales', *Journal of the Royal Statistical Society*, A, 170, Part 4, 891–908.

Stillwell, J. and Duke-Williams, O. (2007). 'Understanding census migration and commuting data', *Journal of the Royal Statistical Society*, A, 170, Part 2, 425–45.

Welsh Assembly Government (2007). *Wales's Population: A Demographic Overview: 1971–2005*, Cardiff, Welsh Assembly Government.

—— (2008a). Llwybro-Routes, *http://www.llwybro-routes.co.uk/*, accessed 4 January 2008.

—— (2008b). *Wales's Population: A Demographic Overview: 2008*, Cardiff, Welsh Assembly Government.

Wilcox, S. (2005). *Affordability and the Intermediate Housing Market*, York, Joseph Rowntree Foundation.

Williams, G. and Morris, D. (2000). *Language Planning and Language Use: Welsh in a Global Age*, Cardiff, University of Wales Press.

Attitudes to Language and Bilingualism among English In-Migrants to North Wales

Howard Davis, Graham Day and Angela Drakakis-Smith
School of Social Sciences
Bangor University

Introduction

The future of the Welsh language is intimately connected with the attitudes, culture, identities and language of those in Wales who do not speak Welsh. This includes the Welsh-born English-speaking population and a substantial minority born outside Wales. This paper is concerned with the latter category: those originating outside Wales who are most likely to define themselves as English or from English backgrounds. The scale of population mobility is substantial. Between 1981 and 1990 some 600,000 people chose to settle in Wales, the vast majority from elsewhere in the UK (Osmond, 1987; Day, 1989). The proportion of English-born people living in Wales has increased steadily in the last fifty years, to more than one in five by 2001. For some, this amounts to a process of Anglicization which asserts an English attitude to language, culture and identity, in opposition to Welsh and Welshness, especially in the Welsh-speaking heartlands of the north and west. In many areas the demographic pressure on the language is reinforced by the out-migration of Welsh speakers for reasons of education and employment. Thus from time to time activists deploy the rhetoric of the rising tide, of 'strangers in our own land' (Jenkins and Williams, 2000: 303), as if defending the Welsh language were a matter of holding back the surge. Cymuned is a recent example (Jones and Fowler 2008; Drakakis-Smith et al., 2008). In reality, as many studies show, prospects for the language depend on a multitude of factors, only some of which are linked to migration, or susceptible to policy initiatives.

Studies of the Welsh language in the twentieth century (Aitchison and Carter, 2000a; Jenkins and Williams, 2000) have concluded that by the 1990s an important turning-point had been reached. By then, public attitudes to the language among non-Welsh-speakers as well as Welsh speakers were overwhelmingly positive. The 1993 Welsh Language Act provided the framework for a variety of measures to promote the language, and the new National Assembly for Wales promised to be able to deliver relevant policies across a range of public institutions, notably education. On the other hand, demographic changes continued to weigh against the survival of Welsh as a community language in rural areas (Cloke et al., 1995). The ongoing decline of religion and the rural economy, both crucial for language maintenance in the past, were grounds for pessimism. Therefore although a number of conditions for positive language shift appeared to have been met, there were still reasons to be sceptical about whether growth in numbers of young, predominantly urban Welsh speakers would compensate for continuing erosion in the heartland communities. While the 2001 Census results confirmed that the total number of Welsh speakers had risen, to 20.8 per cent of the population, reversing the declining trend for the first time in census history, this occurred against a background of demographic changes which included population decline in a third of the Welsh local authority areas, an increase in median age, and further growth in the proportion of people born outside the country.

English Migration and Welsh Language

Although it is widely perceived that English migration has a deleterious impact on Welsh language and culture, relatively little research has been done to examine the issue from the standpoint of the in-migrants themselves. When reference is made, it is often in the context of questions of local economic regeneration, housing (Fevre, Borland and Denney, 1999), tourism (Phillips and Thomas, 2001) or retirement settlement, primarily seen from the viewpoint of the native population. Various commentators have considered the relationships between Welsh locals and in-migrants in rural contexts (Morris, 1989; Symonds, 1990; Day and Murdoch, 1993; Jones, 1993; Cloke et al., 1997; James, 2003). Given the steep decline in the relative importance of the agricultural labour force, these studies naturally focus on alternative strategies for sustaining rural communities and alternative sources of employment in services, small industries and tourism (Wenger, 1980; Day, 2002). Planning for affordable housing in areas of high migration or second-home ownership is a related theme (Bollom, 1978; Johnson, 2003). In such discussions the 'English' (who provide the overwhelming majority of in-migrants to Wales) usually are perceived as alien to Welsh society, its values and sense of identity (Morris, 1989; Cloke et al., 1995; 1997; Jones, 1993). In-migrants from England are viewed typically as having better jobs, being economically better off and more likely to take control than blend into their local community. This is not far from the stereotype of the English as arrogant and intrusive, as discussed for example by Giggs and Pattie (1992); Charles and Davies (1997); Cloke et al. (1998); James (2003); and Robinson and Gardner (2006). Sometimes an alternative stereotype emerges, of older or poorer incomers who are a burden on their recipient communities. In their detailed study of social changes in rural Wales, Cloke et al. (1997) cite the conclusion of Jones (1993) that local people can be severed from their living Welsh culture by an 'influx of Englishness'. Numerous quotations from informants illustrate how this is believed to have happened, and how English people do not 'belong' to Welsh villages, but lead their lives as if they were still in England (Cloke et al., 1997:133, 149). In these portrayals of the English, the Welsh language is seen as a symbol of a society and culture under threat, not as part of a solution to community cohesion and development. Little is said about attitudes amongst the non-Welsh-speaking population, or their level of acceptance of Welsh language and culture.

Given the importance of this theme, it is surprising how little direct evidence exists to show the viewpoints and attitudes of the English who have settled in Wales. This contrasts with a larger volume of writing about the English in Scotland, where they form a much smaller minority (Jedrej and Nuttall, 1996; Burnett, 1998; Watson, 2003; McIntosh et al., 2004). Data on Wales make it difficult to identify the opinions of incomers as a distinct category, suggesting that the English in Wales are among those rural 'others' (Philo, 1992; Milbourne, 1997), whose voices are marginalized through the discourses of Welshness and the Welsh-language minority. There are some relevant, albeit tangential, sources of information, such as evidence on attitudes to the Welsh language among the general population, including in-migrants. The symbolic status and esteem of the language is a determining factor in its vitality. In the view of Aitchison and Carter, leading analysts of language change, there has been a 'revolution' in the status of the language within Wales, marked by its ability to carry social and economic advantages (Aitchison and Carter, 2000b:107). A survey for the Welsh Language Board showed that 71 per cent of the sample supported or strongly supported the use of Welsh and fewer than 4 per cent were opposed. An even larger proportion felt the language was an asset, 88 per cent agreeing that it is 'something to be proud of' (Welsh Language Board, 1995).

Other sources of evidence are fragmentary but quite revealing about the complexity of the relationships between locality, community identity and language. For example, a study of people's experiences of living on low income in rural Wales (Milbourne and Hughes, 2005) found a strong positive sense of attachment to place and to a sense of a community in the area. Most respondents, including in-migrants, considered they were socially embedded in 'their' community, although even after many years some experienced ambivalence. A respondent living in Gwynedd considered that her sense of community belonging varied according to how others in the local area constructed her identity:

> Sometimes I feel as though I belong, other times I don't because I was actually born in Yorkshire you see and Welsh isn't my first language, and here it's very, very Welsh speaking. It's very much a Welsh community and sometimes people can be OK with you, and other times people will not; they'll look at you as if you are an outsider even though I've lived here for 37 years. (Milbourne and Hughes, 2005:30)

Studies of the impact of tourism on language provide another source of evidence. Overall, they emphasize the contribution that tourism makes to the decline of Welsh in tourist areas, both through the use of English as a medium of interaction between tourists and residents, and via the influx of tourism workers (Phillips, 2000; Phillips and Thomas, 2001). Taking into account the impact of retirement settlement in areas which are attractive for tourism (retirees being the group least likely to master a new language), evidence indicates that from a demographic point of view the boundary between

Welsh-speaking Wales and Anglicized Wales is being 'pushed westward' (Aitchison and Carter, 2000a:121) in key areas of north and west Wales. Moreover, there is a close connection between tourism and in-migration. Positive experiences of the environment, social and cultural life as a visitor are an important 'pull' factor in eventual relocation and settlement. For some, the acquaintance is superficial, but for others the desire to settle comes from a genuine sense of attachment to familiar places, people and a perceived higher quality of life.

Adaptation and Language Acquisition among In-Migrants

A small-scale study of in-migration and the Welsh language was undertaken in 1988 in the area of Tregaron, mid-Wales (Aitchison et al., 1989), where the percentage of Welsh speakers had fallen sharply, from 91.5 per cent in 1961 to 76.7 per cent in 1981. Though population remained stable overall in the area during this period, this represented the outcome of significant out-migration of mainly Welsh speakers, combined with a similar level of in-migration, mainly of people born outside Wales (as high as 45.8 per cent in one local community). The study focused mainly on the impact of these trends among school-age children, and the extent to which they acquired and made use of the Welsh language in the home and elsewhere. The apparent success of an educational strategy is reflected by Dyfed Education Authority figures from 1978 showing that just 58.8 per cent of the pupils in Ysgol Uwchradd Tregaron were able to speak Welsh when they first came to the school, whereas by the time of the survey 82.8 per cent were classed as 'fluent' or 'developing fluency' (Aitchison et al., 1989: 9). The authors conclude that education provides the key support for language and for maintaining the cultural environment of Welsh:

> Although the process of immigration is seen by many as constituting a major threat to the language, it has to be said that a substantial number of incomers have made efforts to learn Welsh, and, furthermore, have been happy to see their children become part of the Welsh-speaking community. The fact that high percentages of non-local respondents intend to remain in the area for some time could also bode well for the promotion of the language. The critical issue here seems to be preservation of the cultural environment, so that for the younger members of the community the use of Welsh is simply an unexceptional part of

everyday living and not largely set aside in life outside school. (Aitchison et al., 1989:31)

So demographic changes do not tell the whole story. The study suggests that for in-migrants coming to this area at this time, there was a positive interaction between a robust education policy designed to promote the language, the attitudes held by most incomers and a positive cultural environment embracing the majority of the population. Since then, educational polices have been strengthened and the status of the language (including its perceived economic value) has risen. However, the extent to which incomers in other areas in more recent times have shown the same apparent willingness to integrate has remained largely unexplored.

The Study

To address this gap in knowledge we undertook research during 2005–6 on the attitudes and experiences of in-migrants who had come from England to live in north-west Wales. The area is particularly suitable for such a study: it is part of the Welsh-speaking heartland, with some of the highest proportions of Welsh-speakers in Wales, while at the same time having particularly high concentrations of in-migrants. A challenge in studying the impact of in-migration is to identify the target population correctly. In the public debate, all incomers tend to be treated as a single group, 'the English'. For example, in interviews cited by Cloke et al., respondents routinely elide the categories of 'outsiders', 'foreigners', 'newcomers' and the English (1997:23–7, and *passim*). This tendency to treat the English as a homogeneous group contrasts with the growing sensitivity shown by researchers towards the complexity and differentiation of Welsh identities (Bowie, 1993; Thompson and Day, 1999; Williams, 1999). Our research targeted people originating outside Wales who had moved across its borders from England, without prejudging what they might consider their identity to be.

The study was conducted in selected communities in the county borough of Conwy and in Gwynedd, intended to exemplify significant contrasts within the region. Based on electoral districts, for which reliable demographic data including country of birth and language skills is available from the 2001 Census, they are aligned east to west, from less Welsh-speaking to more Welsh-speaking areas. The three areas chosen were:

(1) A group of relatively 'gentrified' villages in the Conwy Valley (Rowen, Tyn y Groes, Tal y Bont, Llanbedr y Cennin and Dolgarrog), about one-third of whose residents were born in England, although adjacent areas have high proportions of Welsh speakers and people born in Wales.
(2) Three of Gwynedd's former slate quarrying settlements (Bethesda, Rachub and Deiniolen) where the percentage of Welsh speakers is higher and the proportion born in England lower than the other locations.
(3) Three coastal villages on the Llŷn peninsula (Criccieth, Nefyn and Abersoch) with very high concentrations of second homes, which are attractive both to retired people, and younger incomers interested in outdoor activities, yet where nevertheless the majority of residents possess Welsh-language skills.

In each location, a sample was drawn using the electoral register as a sampling frame. For reasons of economy and simplicity, we excluded individuals with what looked like obviously 'Welsh' names (such as Jones, Davies, or Rees). Although it risked leaving out some of the in-migrants, this strategy succeeded in producing a sample that satisfied the definition of in-migrants from England and contained a reasonable cross-section in terms of age, gender, location and length of stay. Information was gathered subsequently in two stages. A profiling questionnaire was administered to a sample of 260 individuals, systematically selected from across the different locations (reflecting a 61.7 per cent response rate). The questionnaire was completed face to face with the researcher or by telephone. Those interviewed ranged in age from under thirty to over seventy, with a preponderance aged over fifty; 42 per cent were men, and 58 per cent women. The general characteristics of our sample profile are described in detail elsewhere (Day et al., forthcoming). Following this a subset of fifty individuals were interviewed in depth about their experiences of migration and integration.

Survey results

Survey answers revealed that incomers did not always conform to the stereotype of the 'English' as outsiders without roots in Wales. Many respondents claimed to have strong attachments to Wales, and some said they had Welsh relatives or Welsh ancestry. Many had visited Wales over a long period of time and developed an affinity to the area in which they had eventually settled, and a significant proportion had lived in Wales for a lengthy period: 42 per cent for more than twenty years, and 70 per cent for more than ten years. Recent arrivals, resident in Wales for three years or less, constituted only a tenth of the sample. Almost 60 per cent had had previous Welsh addresses, two-thirds of them outside the local area. In other words, there had been ample time for most to have made significant adaptations to life in Wales. Furthermore, the majority said that moving to Wales had not presented them with any particular problems. Among the minority who did identify difficulties, 47 per cent thought there was an attitude problem towards newcomers, 23 per cent mentioned anti-English feeling, and 19 per cent referred to a language barrier. When asked specifically to think about negative aspects of living in Wales, only 11 per cent of the entire sample referred to anti-English feeling, and 5 per cent mentioned the Welsh language.

When asked to describe their identity, only a minority (26.5 per cent) identified themselves as 'English'. A larger proportion (45.4 per cent) claimed 'British' identity, with others identifying themselves as Welsh (7.7 per cent), European (6.2 per cent), Welsh/British (1.5 per cent) and English/Welsh (1.9 per cent). This suggests that in-migrants from England may be more prepared to adopt a hybrid or inclusive identity than they would in a more English setting. The idea that people might have adapted their identities as a result of living in Wales is discussed more fully elsewhere (Day et al., 2006).

The information on attitudes to language and language skills was based on reported language learning, use of Welsh and general attitudes to the bilingual environment. Nearly half of the sample (48.8 per cent) reported that they had learnt some Welsh. The remaining respondents were asked why they had not learnt Welsh (see Table 1). Some volunteered information that they were not competent linguists, that they were dyslexic, or too old. Significantly, among the respondents who had 'not learned' were some who had been to classes and tried to learn – even making several attempts. At the community level, scores for participation in Welsh learning were highest in Nefyn (77.8 per cent), Rachub (60.0 per cent) and Bethesda (58.3 per cent), and lowest in Deiniolen (29.4 per cent). The main reasons offered for not learning the language were its 'difficulty', and that it was not perceived as necessary. Problems of access to learning opportunities were not mentioned.

Table 1 Reasons given for not learning Welsh

Reason	%
Too difficult	38.1
Not really necessary	33.1
No time	15.0
Laziness	6.3
No particular reason	3.8
Lack of encouragement	2.5
Too expensive	0.6
Lack of confidence	0.6

Respondents who had learnt Welsh were asked how much they used the language. Among this group, 6.8 per cent claimed to use Welsh all the time, 51.4 per cent said sometimes, 18.9 per cent 'rarely' and 23.0 per cent 'never'. Respondents who said they used Welsh all the time were found only in three communities, with Rachub and Bethesda having the highest percentages (15.8 and 20.0 per cent respectively). In all the communities there were respondents saying they sometimes used Welsh, the highest scores occurring in Rowen (70.0 per cent), Bethesda (66.7 per cent), Abersoch (56.3 per cent) and Criccieth (46.7 per cent). Likewise there were respondents in every community who said they never used their Welsh.

Respondents were then asked in what circumstances they used the Welsh language (see Table 2).

The strong impression from these data is that for the learners of Welsh as a second language, the contexts of use are more likely to be 'public' (in work, and interaction with friends and neighbours) than 'private' (within the family). This of course is the reverse of the pattern of use in traditional language communities where the language is under threat and the home is the last refuge. When asked if there was anyone else in the family who spoke Welsh, 54.5 per cent of our sample replied positively. Family members included children, grandchildren, spouses and other relatives.

Given the great importance of family and education in the processes of language transmission, further questions were asked about both. Of those respondents who had children, 50.5 per cent

Table 2 If you have learned Welsh, where do you use it?

Where spoken	%
At work	28.0
With friends	18.0
With neighbours	17.0
Shopping	13.0
Greetings	11.0
With family	5.0
With children	5.0
On the phone	3.0

stated that one or more of their children had been brought up in Wales. The highest percentages were for Bethesda (70.8 per cent) and Nefyn (48.1 per cent), and the lowest were Rowen (27.3 per cent) and Abersoch (25.7 per cent). So far as children of school age were concerned, it was found that numbers attending a local junior school were highest in Rachub, Bethesda, and Criccieth. Some children (12.6 per cent of those of school age) attended schools elsewhere in the area – usually non-Welsh-medium, independent or boarding schools. This gives a general indication of the relative size of the next generation gaining exposure to Welsh through the educational context. The next question sought to discover where children above school age were now living, if not living with the respondent. Of those in this category, 22.9 per cent had remained in the local area, another 7.2 per cent remained in Wales, 52.2 per cent lived elsewhere in the UK and 16.5 per cent lived abroad. This provides an indication of the extent of out-migration of younger people from in-migrant homes in the area. There is no information as to whether they will join the ranks of returners in future. More members of the next generation were still living in the local area in the communities of Rachub, Bethesda and Deiniolen, whereas Dolgarrog, Criccieth, Abersoch and Nefyn had fewest. The figures tend to confirm that the 'normalization' of Welsh language amongst in-migrant families is greater in the former quarrying areas, where the proportion of Welsh speakers is high and rates of retirement settlement are low.

Altogether, our survey findings suggested that in-migrants take a generally positive position on their identity within Wales (Day et al., 2006). They do not set out deliberately to maintain a distinct migrant community or culture. They are not inclined to view themselves as part of any 'problem' or sharp division on cultural or linguistic lines. Most adopt a broadly sympathetic and supportive attitude towards the Welsh language and culture, and readily accept the consequences of this for their children's passage through the schooling system. Such attitudes are in marked contrast to the overwhelmingly negative stance adopted by in-migrants in some earlier studies (Morris, 1989), suggesting there may have been some significant shifts in the climate of opinion. However, only about half of the adults had been prepared to take up the challenge of learning Welsh, with relatively few succeeding at more than a basic level. For a more complete understanding of how these attitudes to Welsh language and culture work we need to consider data from the fifty qualitative interviews.

Views on Language and Culture

Interview material confirmed the findings of previous research, that there is a high level of support for the Welsh language throughout the population. However, the attitudes expressed by English in-migrants do not necessarily fit neatly into a spectrum from positive to negative, as simple attitude scale data might suggest. Much depends on their understanding of the place of the Welsh language in the society and culture of Wales. Tolerance for a language seen as belonging essentially to others carries different implications from the idea of language as a significant cultural legacy open to all, or an instrumental view of language as an opportunity to be grasped as a potential business or employment asset. Interview data allow these different inflections to be identified and the relationships between them explored.

Interviewees were prompted to express themselves under the general theme 'How do you feel about living in a bilingual community?' and 'Do you have a view of bilingualism?' Responses could be checked and compared with the answers to another question in the section on education: 'How do you feel about teaching in Welsh?' The most positive responses to bilingualism take other cultures and languages as their reference point. This 'cosmopolitan' attitude treats competence in the two languages as normal, a necessity and not a matter of choice.

> This is Wales, children should learn Welsh and the Welsh language should be kept up. I agree with that ... I think everybody should be

bilingual and when you move you should at least make an effort to learn the language. In any other country you would. (Interview 15)

Before I had my child I wasn't sure about it. But it's fine. He's seven and his English is poor compared to his Welsh but that will change. He doesn't have a problem at all and he likes the language. I'm going to have a language tutor once a week to help him along with English but that's my choice. If we were in France it would be the same. (Interview 21)

On this basis, one interviewee would even accept an element of coercion: 'I think [bilingualism] is essential. It must be.'

Q. Should the Welsh be more forceful in making it the language of Wales?
R. I would say not too forceful as that might put some people off. Just a gentle persuasion might do the trick.
Q. Perhaps forceful is too strong a word. There is this politeness, perhaps there should be less of that?
R. Yes. I had a relation who went to France and the French wouldn't speak in English, they had to learn . . . I think the Welsh are a bit too tolerant and perhaps they should make people learn it in a nice sort of way . . . The British [sic] are terrible with languages. At least the Welsh speak two languages. (Interview 6)

The majority of responses either expressed approval for bilingualism or conveyed the idea that bilingualism in Wales is a necessity. The main context for debating these opinions is not interaction within the adult world of work, or even everyday interaction with neighbours or friends, but the education system and the rightness or otherwise of requiring children to be schooled in both languages.

I'm all for [bilingualism]. The local school is basically a Welsh-language school . . . Most of the children who go to the school pick up Welsh really well. And speak it fluently enough at eleven to go to the Welsh-medium secondary school if they want to. Some children are moved away by their parents because they feel that their English is suffering or because they are afraid that if they don't speak Welsh themselves that they won't be able to help with the homework or know what's going on at school. Apart from that – yep. (Interview 12)

Some argued that the choice is not purely individual, since a community is responsible for how its children are taught.

I think it should be truly bilingual. In a culture where you've got a living language then kids should be able to communicate in their own language . . . if it's true bilingualism I haven't got a problem with that. (Interview 10)

If the community wants its children to be brought up Welsh-speaking then fine. No problem with that. (Interview 34)

It's a Welsh choice again. The children speak Welsh until they are five or six and English as a second language. That's fine as long as Wales can back up the opportunities for Welsh speakers for employment which obviously they will do. (Interview 32)

Not all respondents had children who had been through the system, so their views were not necessarily based on experience but on perceptions coloured by their understanding of the significance of schooling (and possibly their own experiences of adult learning).

I don't think teaching them Welsh does any harm. Children of primary school age pick things up very quickly – any language, not just Welsh and English. If people are coming here to live I think they must be aware that they are coming to a Welsh area and it's better for the children to learn Welsh. It will benefit them. (Interview 41)

A broader comparison of languages supports more complex accounts of the relationship between Welsh and English, including awareness that speakers of both languages may experience mobility, and that outside Wales English has a comparative advantage.

I think there should be more emphasis on bilingualism at primary school level, a lot more Welsh than there is at present . . . I'd have been concerned if there was Welsh only at primary level. But I wouldn't now . . . I do still feel that English is an important language to have under your belt. I don't think it should be excluded . . . it's very insular to think that everybody born and brought up in Wales is going to remain in Wales . . . If you already have people questioning the validity of an A Level in Welsh as a foreign language in English universities then something is going wrong. (Interview 4)

It's a good thing to maintain the Welsh language, definitely. People speaking Welsh around me doesn't bother me. I've worked abroad where I couldn't understand the language anyway. It's fairly essential but I don't think it should be pushed to the detriment of English where youngsters are well educated in Welsh and they have to go out in the big wide world. The international language is English. It could be a disadvantage to some youngsters. The more intelligent ones pick up both languages and it's not a problem. The others hang around here, don't go to college. It doesn't do them any favours. (Interview 18)

If that's what the family chooses . . . If children are never going to cross the border that's fine but these days you have to think big. It's the global village. You can retain your identity but you have to speak to the rest of the world as well. (Interview 42)

Only a minority of the interviewees expressed scepticism towards Welsh, and never with great passion. This minority perspective involved an element of inconsistency, combining a sentimental view of the language as an attractive cultural legacy with an instrumental view seeing it as an obstacle in certain circumstances.

I don't think Welsh is very useful to the Welsh children. French and German would be better . . . It's nice historically to have the Welsh language. I was quite shocked when I saw that to get a job in nursing you have to speak Welsh. I'm sure most of the doctors and patients speak English. But if it's a policy, fair enough. (Interview 22)

If I had kids would I want them to go to a bilingual school? That's a difficult one . . . if they could learn from an early age then I wouldn't mind but if they were ten or eleven it would be more of an imposition. I think English opens up more opportunities than Welsh. Even the Welsh poets like Dylan Thomas wrote in English . . . the benefits of learning Welsh are mainly to be seen in terms of socializing and mixing and being able to get jobs in the civil service . . . but children may not stay in Wales. (Interview 40)

In a rare exception to the rule that the Welsh language is accepted as an inescapable feature of the local landscape, one individual admitted turning a blind eye to the language, owing to its supposed link with nationalism: 'I never think about [bilingualism]. I'm quite happy in my ignorance . . . I think it's very divisive actually. I don't like this nationalism thing they're trying to promote all the time' (Interview 50).

There is a link between national sentiment, political nationalism and Welsh language of course, but each can exist independently of the other. Most respondents did not make this connection, but referred instead to the development of Wales as a nation in the context of devolution, the Welsh Assembly and the positive growth of public institutions and awareness.

Q. Has the National Assembly been a good thing for Wales?
R. Yes, I do think it's made people think of Wales as a separate country more. We've actually got an Assembly.
Q. Has it given people more confidence?

R. I think it's one of the factors. There are a lot of things that have made people a bit more confident about being Welsh. The Assembly, the growing number of people who are speaking Welsh. In the entertainment world actors are quite proud to say they are Welsh now, pop groups and visual signs everywhere – TV, radio. There has also been a lot of development in the language. It means that Wales feels different from England.
Q. Is that resented?
R. Not among the people I come across. I'm sure it does happen. But no, I think people who come here . . . come because it's different. (Interview 12)

From the above responses it appears that the majority either approves of bilingualism or can be persuaded of its merits. Another section of the interview focused on experiences in the community, and in-migrants' level of engagement with 'Welsh' activities, including whether language is perceived as a means or a barrier to integration. Although few respondents could claim to be bilingual this did not prevent a significant number from joining in with Welsh-medium or bilingual activities (like eisteddfod, music, or church). Overall, 46 per cent said that they did not get involved, but 20 per cent said that they did, whilst 32 per cent said that they had either been involved in the past or they were involved via children, but otherwise probably would not be. People living in the Conwy Valley were more likely to take part in 'Welsh' activities (as they defined them) than those living in the other areas. The diversity of their experiences is shown in the following responses, which are also notable for the importance attached to personal connections and the development of these relationships over time:

> We get involved with Welsh people rather than Welsh things. Because we're doing the same things as they are, WI etc. (Interview 2)

> We went to the eisteddfod when the children were competing, the children attend the chapel Sunday school so I attend the services. I still do that. One child does the Sunday school. (Interview 4)

> Yes, I go to the eisteddfods. Before we went to things because they were Welsh. Now we go to things because we want to go to them and they're Welsh. There's so much going on we have to choose. (Interview 12)

> I used to sing in the choir here. We're involved in different societies both Welsh and English. (Interview 30)

Some respondents, when asked about taking part in local Welsh activities, indicated that the divide between Welsh and English is too great to overcome readily. But this was interpreted as a personal matter, not something incompatible with general sympathy or support for bilingualism. Particularly where children's activities are involved, the two cultures were held to overlap.

> I did have a chance to go to a couple of things but they're all in Welsh so I didn't see the point. There are quite a lot of things I'd like to do but it's all in Welsh . . . But there's always something in English. (Interview 22)

> I would say yes and no. We sat through many a competition at the eisteddfodau when our children were at school. It's not something I would want to go to myself. It's probably too Welsh culture for me. I think Welsh people join in a lot especially when their children are very young. But when they get a bit older it becomes more middle-class and . . . the educated Welsh. (Interview 41)

Dismissive comments about Welsh culture among the in-migrants were rare. However, evidence is limited by the fact that the sample is weighted towards the older age groups and their experiences of child rearing. There are no significant data on the experience of sporting activities, media consumption or participation in popular music events, which are likely to be more widespread among young adults. The markers of 'Welshness' in these activities may be very different from more traditional cultural markers, like eisteddfodau or choirs.

Conclusion

Attitudes to questions of language and bilingualism have been explored through the responses of a sample selected to be broadly representative of English in-migrants to three areas of north-west Wales. The conclusions that can be drawn complement the existing, census-based studies of language change conducted in recent decades with reference to the Welsh heartlands, *Y Fro Gymraeg*. They confirm that prospects for the normalization of Welsh language are better in the areas where demographic pressures (especially in the form of concentrations of retirees) are more moderate. Our results are generally consistent with census findings that point to the rate of erosion of Welsh as a community language being greatest in areas where the proportion of incomers and second-home ownership is highest. Although attitudes to the Welsh language among English in-migrants are generally positive, and there are opportunities to participate in language learning and 'Welsh' activities in such communities, the incentive is reduced by the relative ease of local access to predominantly English communication and culture. Conversely, where settlement in Wales is linked more closely to employment, family and 'other' reasons, and where demographic pressures are somewhat lower, as in the former quarrying settlements, the opportunities and incentives to integrate are greater. The findings also confirm that education provides the key institution for the integration of the younger generation and their acquisition of the Welsh language. As shown by the earlier study of Tregaron (Aitchison et al., 1989), English parents support bilingual learning with very few reservations. A bilingual environment is accepted as a fact of life in these areas, and is more likely to be welcomed than resisted. Typically, Wales is seen as an emerging European nation, sharing the diversity of language and culture that many of its neighbours take for granted. Only a small minority appear to regard Welsh language and culture as anachronistic or as having only residual, touristic value.

In terms of language policy and planning, the study's implications are strongly positive for strategies of bilingual education, equality of recognition in the workplace and efforts to support language transmission in families where Welsh is not the primary medium of communication. It does, however, highlight the gap between the general willingness of English incomers to face the challenge of learning Welsh and the failure of many to achieve a standard that would allow them to communicate readily and sustainably within the Welsh language community. The mechanisms for language learning are clearly in place and accessible. In the wider context of the UK's poor performance in language education, the figure of nearly half of the sample undertaking some form of learning in Welsh is a very positive sign of the propensity to engage. The problem is how to take this willingness and find ways to facilitate learning at the next stage, so that basic skills are embedded in everyday interaction, reinforced and encouraged to develop. The same message emerges from a qualitative study of newcomers on the Llŷn peninsula conducted for the Welsh Language Board and Gwynedd Council. This found that 'there was a lack of informal methods of learning Welsh and this was a problem ...[learners] did not feel that were enough informal networks or activities available to practise and learn Welsh' (Welsh Language Board, 2003: 6). If such barriers can be overcome, then there is the prospect of a virtuous circle developing between the strategies and processes of language maintenance which have helped to slow the decline of Welsh in the heartlands, and the parallel processes that are encouraging language regeneration in areas and among populations that have not previously been identified with the Welsh core.

Notes

[1] Funded by the Social Science Committee of the University of Wales Board of Celtic Studies.

References

Aitchison, J. and Carter, H. (2000a). *Language, Economy and Society: The Changing Fortunes of the Welsh Language in the Twentieth Century*, Cardiff, University of Wales Press.

—— (2000b). 'The Welsh language 1921–1991: a geolinguistic perspective', in G. Jenkins and M. Williams (eds.), *'Let's do our best for the ancient tongue': The Welsh Language in the Twentieth Century*, Cardiff, University of Wales Press, pp. 29–107.

Aitchison, J., Carter, J. and Rogers, D. (1989). *Inmigration and the Welsh Language: A Case Study of Tregaron and its Region*, Rural Surveys Research Unit Monograph No. 3, Aberystwyth, University College of Wales.

Bollom, C. (1978). *Attitudes and Second Homes in Rural Wales*, Cardiff, University of Wales, Board of Celtic Studies.

Bowie, F. (1993). 'Wales from within: conflicting interpretations of Welsh identity', in S. Macdonald (ed.), *Inside European Identities: Ethnography in Western Europe*, Oxford, Berg, pp. 167–93.

Burnett, K. (1998). 'Local heroics: reflecting on incomers and local rural development discourses in Scotland', *Sociologia Ruralis*, 38, 2, 204–23.

Charles, N. and Davies, C. A. (1997). 'Contested communities: the refuge movement and cultural identities in Wales', *Sociological Review*, 45, 3, 416–36.

Cloke, P., Goodwin, M. and Milbourne, P. (1995). '"There's so many strangers in the village now": marginalization and change in 1990s Welsh rural life-styles', *Contemporary Wales*, 8, 47–74.

—— (1997). *Rural Wales: Community and Marginalization*, Cardiff, University of Wales Press.

—— (1998) 'Inside looking out: different experiences of cultural competences in rural lifestyles', in P. Boyle and K. Halfacree (eds.), *Migration into Rural Areas*, Chichester, Wiley, pp. 134–50.

Day, G. (1989). 'A million on the move? Population change and rural Wales', *Contemporary Wales*, 3, 137–60.

—— (2002). *Making Sense of Wales*, Cardiff, University of Wales Press.
—— (2006). *Community and Everyday Life*, London, Routledge.
Day, G., Davis, H. and Drakakis-Smith, A. (2006). 'Being English in north Wales: inmigration and the inmigrant experience', *Nationalism and Ethnic Politics*, 12, 3–4, 577–98.
—— (forthcoming). '"There's one shop you don't go into if you are English": the social and political integration of English in-migrants into Wales', *Journal of Ethnic and Migration Studies*.
Day, G. and Murdoch, J. (1993). 'Locality and community: coming to terms with place', *Sociological Review*, 41, 1, 82–111.
Drakakis-Smith, A., Day, G. and Davis, H. (2008). 'Portrait of a locality? The local press at work in north-west Wales 2000–2005', *Contemporary Wales*, 21, 25–46.
Fevre, R., Borland, J. and Denney, D. (1999). 'Nation, community and conflict: housing policy and immigration in north Wales', in R. Fevre and A. Thompson, *Nation, Identity and Social Theory*, Cardiff, University of Wales Press, pp. 129–48.
Giggs, J. and Pattie, C. (1992). 'Wales as a plural society', *Contemporary Wales*, 5, 25–63.
James, E. (2003). 'Research on your own doorstep: Welsh rural communities and the perceived effects of in-migration', in C. A. Davies and S. Jones (eds.), *Welsh Communities: New Ethnographic Perspectives*, Cardiff, University of Wales Press, pp. 49–79.
Jedrej, C. and Nuttall, M. (1996). *White Settlers: The Impact of Rural Repopulation in Scotland*, Luxemburg, Harwood Academic Publishers.
Jenkins, G. and Williams, M. (eds.) (2000). *'Let's do our best for the ancient tongue': The Welsh Language in the Twentieth Century*, Cardiff, University of Wales Press.
Johnson E. (2003). *A Source of Contention: Affordable Housing in Rural Wales*, Cardiff, Institute of Welsh Affairs.
Jones, N. (1993). *Living in Rural Wales*, Llandysul, Gomer Press.
Jones, R. and Fowler C. (2008). *Placing the Nation: Aberystwyth and the Reproduction of Welsh Nationalism*, Cardiff, University of Wales Press.
McIntosh, I., Sim, D. and Robertson, D. (2004). 'We hate the English, except for you, cos you're our pal: identification of the English in Scotland', *Sociology*, 38, 1, 43–60.
Milbourne, P. (ed.) (1997). *Revealing Rural Others: Representation, Power and Identity in the British Countryside*, London, Pinter.
Milbourne, P. and Hughes, R. (2005). *Poverty and Social Exclusion in Rural Wales*, Research Report 6, Aberystwyth, Wales Rural Observatory.
Morris, D. (1989). 'Language contact and social networks in Ynys Môn', *Contemporary Wales*, 3, 99–117.
Osmond, J. (1987). 'A million on the move', *Planet*, 62, 114–18.
Phillips, D. (2000). 'We'll keep a welcome? The effects of tourism on the Welsh language', in G. Jenkins and M. Williams (eds.), *'Let's do our best for*

the ancient tongue': *The Welsh Language in the Twentieth Century*, Cardiff, University of Wales Press, pp. 527–50.

Phillips, D. and Thomas, C. (2001). *The Effects of Tourism on the Welsh Language in North-West Wales*, Aberystwyth, University of Wales Centre for Advanced Celtic Studies.

Philo, C. (1992). 'Neglected rural geographies: a review', *Journal of Rural Studies*, 8, 193–207.

Robinson, V. and Gardner, H. (2006). 'Place matters: exploring the distinctiveness of racism in rural Wales', in S. Neal and J. Agyeman (eds.), *The New Countryside? Ethnicity, Nation and Exclusion in Contemporary Rural Britain*, Bristol, Policy Press, 73–98.

Symonds, A. (1990). 'Migrations, communities and social change', in R. Jenkins and A. Edwards (eds.), *One Step Forward? South and West Wales towards the Year 2000*, Llandysul, Gomer, pp. 21–34.

Thompson A. and Day, G. (1999). 'Situating Welshness: "local" experience and national identity', in R. Fevre and A. Thompson, *National Identity and Social Theory: Perspectives from Wales*, Cardiff, University of Wales Press, pp. 27–47.

Watson, M. (2003). *Being English in Scotland*, Edinburgh, Edinburgh University Press.

Welsh Language Board (1995). *Public Attitudes to the Welsh Language*, Research report prepared by NOP Social and Political for the Central Office of Information and the Welsh Language Board, London, NOP Social and Political.

—— (2003). *Research on Newcomers: Qualitative Research*, Cardiff, Beaufort Research Ltd.

Wenger, G. C. (1980). *Mid Wales: Deprivation or Development?* Cardiff, University of Wales Press.

Williams, C. (1999). 'Passports to Wales? Race, nation and identity', in R. Fevre and A. Thompson, *National Identity and Social Theory: Perspectives From Wales* Cardiff, University of Wales Press, 69–89.

Index

Abersoch 154, 156, 157
Aberystwyth 82, 86, 87, 88, 94, 95, 97, 128
Aitchison, J. 149, 151, 152, 164
Amlwch 54, 56, 83, 86, 87, 88, 93, 94, 95, 96, 98
Ammanford 54, 83, 87, 88, 89, 93, 94, 95, 96, 98
Anglesey 128, 129
Annual Review of Sociology ix
Arendt, H. 23
Arfon 122
Audit Commission 56
Auroux, S. 14
Australia 67
Authier, J. 24

Bailey, N. 142
Baker, Colin 3–4, 61–77
Bakhtin, Mikhail 14, 22
Bala 82, 83, 86, 87, 88, 93–4, 95–6, 97
Ball, M. J. 103, 105
Bangor 54, 55, 56, 128
Barron-Hauwaert, S. 65
Bates, E. A. 100
Bellin, W. 105, 107, 110, 111
Belot, M. 137
Berko, J. 104
Bethesda 154, 155, 156, 157
Bhaskar, R. 12
Bialystok, E. 68, 101–2
bilingual schools 62–3, 82, 83–4, 86, 111
bilingualism x, 3–4, 5, 27, 32, 36, 37, 38, 39, 40–1, 43, 44–5, 46–7, 48, 49–50, 51, 54, 55, 58, 61–79, 80, 85, 86, 89, 92, 102, 104, 108–12, 113, 114, 155, 158–63, 164
Blackaby, D. 142
Blunkett, David 51
Bollom, C. 150
Borland, J. 149
Boschma, R. A. 26
Bourdieu, P. 12
Bowie, F. 153
Brassett-Grundy, A. 124
Breton language 105–6
Bührig, Kristin 17
Burnett, K. 150

Caernarvonshire, former county 128
Caerphilly County Council 44
Canada 41, 64, 67, 70
Cardiff 82, 144
Cardiff County Council 44
Cardigan 54, 56, 83, 86, 87, 88, 93, 94, 95–6, 97
Cardiganshire, former county 128
Carmarthen 122
Carmarthen County Council 44
Carmarthen Health Board 44
Carmarthenshire 128, 129, 130
Carter, H. 149, 151, 152
Carter, R. 27
Catalan language 55
Catalonia 54
Census (1971) 121, 124; (1981) 118, 120, 121, 124, 129; (1991) 118, 119, 120, 121, 124, 127, 129, 143; (2001) 5, 55, 118, 119, 120, 121, 127, 130, 137, 142, 144, 149, 153

Central Office of Information 44, 49, 50
Centre for European Research, Wales 54
Ceredigion 122, 129, 130
Ceredigion County Council 56
Charles, N. 150
Child Support Agency 44, 49
Chomsky, Noam 14, 100
Clarke, Charles 51
Clinton, Bill 7
Cloke, P. 149, 150, 153
Content and Language Integrated Learning (CLIL) 77
Conwy 153
Conwy County Council 44, 45
Conwy Valley 154, 162
Cook, V. J. 66
Cooke, P. N. 31
Criccieth 154, 156, 157
Culioli, A. 18, 24–5
Cymdeithas yr Iaith Gymraeg 36
Cymru'n Creu 30
Cymuned 148–9
Cynon valley 82

Dafis, C. 143
Davies, C. A. 150
Davies, D. G. 105, 111
Davis, Howard 5–6, 148–67
Day, Graham 5–6, 143, 148–67
Deiniolen 154, 155, 157
Deleuze, Gilles 22
Denney, D. 149
Department for Work and Pensions (DWP) 44, 49, 50
diglossia 29, 54, 65, 70
Dinefwr 122
Disability and Careers Service 44, 49, 50
Dolgarrog 154, 157
Donovan, N. 137, 142
Dorian, N. 104
Drakakis-Smith, Angela 5–6, 148–67
Drinkwater, S. 142
dual language schools 63, 65, 66, 69, 72, 75, 77

Dwyfor 122
Dyfed 122, 128
Dyfed Education Authority 152

Economics and Sociology Section (University of Wales Guild of Graduates) 1
education x, xi, 2, 3–6, 27–9, 40, 41, 59, 61–79, 81–4, 86, 97, 114, 118, 127, 143, 144, 152–3, 157, 158, 159, 160, 164
Education Reform Act (1988) 127
Edwards, V. 71
Eilers, R. E. 110
eisteddfodau 65, 162, 163
Elman, J. L. 100
England 27, 119–20, 121, 122, 123, 127, 130–1, 133–4, 135, 136, 137, 144, 145, 150, 153, 153, 154, 155, 162
English, the 5, 148–64
English language 3, 4, 5, 27, 32, 39, 46, 47, 53, 55, 61, 62–3, 64, 65, 66, 67, 68, 69, 70, 71, 73, 74, 75, 76, 85, 86–7, 88–93, 94–5, 97, 104, 108, 109, 110, 111, 112, 150, 151, 159, 160, 161
English-medium schools 82, 83, 84, 86
Enlightenment, the 13
Equality and Human Rights Commission 3, 57
Ermisch, J. 137
Estyn 56
European Union (EU) 9, 10, 30–1, 57

Fevre, R. 149
Finland 38, 41, 59
Fishguard 83, 86, 87, 88, 89, 93–4, 95, 96, 98
Fishman, Joshua ix, x, 29, 65, 75
Florida, R. 8
Fodor, J. A. 100
Follath, E. 8
Fordism 21
Foucault, M. 18, 20–1, 22
Fowler, C. 149

Index

Franik, M. 107
'From Act to Action' 56–7

Gaelic Language (Scotland) Act (2005) 50
Gaeltacht, the 42, 65
García, Ofelia 75
Gardner, H. 150
Garfinkel, H. 19
Gathercole, V. C. Mueller 100, 102, 103, 105, 106, 107, 108–9, 111, 112
Giddens, A. 12–13
Giggs, J. 150
Glasgow 50
globalization 2, 8, 9, 11, 16, 30, 32
Goodluck, H. 101
Grosjean, F. 66, 67
Gujarati 51
Gwynedd 122, 128, 129, 130, 151, 153, 154
Gwynedd County Council 44, 45, 46, 58, 164

Hart, B. 110
Hatton, L. 105, 107, 110, 111
Hayek, F. A. 15–16, 17
Hebrew 103, 108
Hechter, Michael ix–x
Hickey, T. 76
Hodgson, G. M. 15
Hoff, E. 100, 102
Home Office 44, 49, 50, 51, 52
Hong Kong 72
Hughes, R. 151

Iaith Pawb 36, 58, 80
Internal Colonialism: The Celtic Fringe in British Development ix–x
International Journal of Bilingual Education and Bilingualism 77
International Journal of the Sociology of Language x, 1
Ireland ix, x, 27, 38, 41–2, 49, 58, 59, 65
Irish language 41–2, 105–6
Italian 103

Jackson, K. 102–3
Jacobson, Rodolfo 72, 73–4, 77
Jaffe, A. 72
James, E. 150
Jedrej, C. 150
Jenkins, G. 148, 149
Jobcentre Plus 44, 49, 50
Johnson, E. 150
Jones, B. M. 104, 105, 107
Jones, G. W. 143
Jones, Hywel M. x, 5–6, 118–47
Jones, K. 129
Jones, M. C. 103, 104, 107
Jones, N. 150
Jones, R. 148–9

knowledge economy x, xi, 1–2, 6, 7–35

Lacan, Jacques 10
Lampeter 82, 83, 86, 87, 88, 94, 95, 97, 128
language acquisition 4, 5–6, 18–19, 65, 99–114, 152–3, 164
Language Action Plan areas 82
language-awareness training 46–7, 50, 56, 58, 59
language learning 4, 5, 27–30, 100–14, 71, 143, 155–6, 158, 160, 164
language legislation 2–3, 6, 36–60; *see also* Welsh Language Act (1993)
language maintenance 2, 12, 29, 64, 149, 152, 164
language officers 48, 50, 51
language planning x, xi, 2–3, 13, 27–8, 29–31, 38, 56, 59, 64, 65, 74, 75, 98, 102, 164
language policy ix, x, xi, 3, 36, 37, 38–9, 43, 45, 53, 57–8, 59, 61, 69, 70, 72, 75, 76, 102, 143, 149, 153, 161, 164
language politics 36, 41, 45, 51, 53, 57, 67, 75, 76
language-practice training 47
language purity 2, 14, 28, 64
language regeneration 144, 164

language rights 3, 6, 30, 37, 38, 39, 40–1, 42, 54, 58
language separation 63, 64–6, 67, 68, 69–72, 75, 76–7
language shift 2, 12, 29, 56, 65, 149
language skills 2, 46, 58, 59, 75, 86, 144, 153, 154, 155, 164
language status 3, 6, 53, 57–8, 65, 72, 74, 75, 125, 151, 153
language use 4, 5, 6, 13, 15, 17–19, 21, 22, 24, 25, 26, 28–30, 42, 45, 47, 54–6, 61–78, 80–98, 118–19, 151, 152–3, 155, 156, 157
Legislative Competence Order for the Welsh Language 57
Levy, Y. 108
Lewis, W. G. 62, 69, 76
Lin, Amy 72
Lindholm-Leary, K. J. 63
Livingston, M. 142
Llanbedr y Cennin 154
Llandysul 83, 86, 87, 88, 93, 94, 95–6, 97
Llanelli 122
Llangefni 83, 86, 87, 88, 94, 95, 97
Llanishen (Cardiff) 49
Llanrwst 83–4, 86, 87, 88, 89, 93, 94, 95–6, 97
Llwybro-Routes project 143
Llŷn peninsula 154, 164
London 49, 50, 111

Machynlleth 54, 84, 86, 87, 88–9, 93, 94, 95–6, 97
McIntosh, I. 150
MacWhinney, B. 100
Marx, Karl 23
Mayr, Robert 4–5, 99–117
Meirionnydd 122
Meisel, Jürgen M. 72
Merionethshire 128
migration 30, 118, 119, 121, 123, 144, 149
  in-migration x, 5, 6, 62, 69, 83, 85, 97, 98, 119, 121, 128–30, 137, 142, 144, 145, 148–64
  internal migration 122, 144

out-migration x, 5, 6, 118–45, 148, 152, 157
return migration 143
Milbourne, P. 150, 151
Minimalism (Chomsky) 100
Moore, D. 72
Morris, Delyth x, xi, 1–6, 80–98, 129, 150, 158
Müller, N. 103
Murdoch, J. 150

National Assembly for Wales 6, 36, 37, 38, 39, 53, 54, 57, 149, 161
National Curriculum 81
Nefyn 154, 155, 157
Nelson, R. R. 16–17
Newcastle 49
Nippold, M. A. 107
Nonaka, I. 25
North Wales Police 44, 45, 46, 48, 52, 58
Nuttall, M. 150

Ó Baoill, D. 106
Ó Cuirreáin, Seán 42
Ofercat Project 55
Office for National Statistics 121
Official Languages Act (Ireland; 2003) 41–2
Official Languages Commission (Ireland) 42
Oller, D. K. 110
ONS Longitudinal Study (LS) 119, 121, 123–4, 127
OPOL 65–6, 70
Osmond, J. 148

Parrino, A. 76
Pattie, C. 150
Pêcheux, M. 19
Pembroke National Park Authority 44
Pembrokeshire 123
Pension Service 44, 49, 50
Phillips, D. 149, 151
Philo, C. 150
Pinker, S. 100, 101, 107
Powell, W. W. 8

Index

Prague School 14
Putnam, R. D. 142
Pwllheli 84, 86, 87, 88, 93, 94, 95–6, 97

Quah, D. 16

Rachub 154, 155, 156, 157
Raymer, J. 143
Reich, Robert 7–8
Reversing Language Shift (Fishman) 29
Rhondda valley 82
Rhwydiaith 46
Rhymni valley 82
Richard Commission 53
Risley, T. 110
Robinson, V. 150
Roeper, T. 101
Romero, M. 76
Rowen 154, 156, 157
Ruthin 54, 55

Saussure, Ferdinand de 13, 14
Schumpeter, Joseph 15
Scotland 50, 150
Scottish Gaelic 104
Sheffield 49
Single Equality Measure 3, 57
Snellman, K. 8
Sociology of Welsh, The (Glyn Williams) 1
Sondag, N. 107
Spanish 103, 110
Sporl, G. 8
Stephens, J. 106
Student Loan Agency 50
Stumper, B. 107
Symonds, A. 150
Szagun, G. 107

Takeuchi, H. 25
Tal y Bont 154
Tallerman, M. 102–3
Taylorism 8, 21
ten Thije, Jan D. 17
Thomas, C. 149, 151
Thomas, Dylan 161

Thomas, Enlli Môn 4–5, 99–117
Thomas, P. W. 103
Thomas, Roy 1
Thompson, A. 153
Tomasello, M. 100, 101, 105
Touraine, A. 9
Transformational Grammar (Chomsky) 100
translanguaging 74–5
Tregaron 152, 164
Tyn y Groes 154

United Kingdom (UK) 27, 37, 38, 49, 57, 58, 67, 119, 121, 128, 148, 157, 164
United Nations 40–1
United States (US) ix, x, 3, 7, 62, 63, 66, 67, 69, 70, 71, 75
Universal Grammar (UG) 100, 101
University of Wales 1, 128
Urdu 51

Van der Walt, C. 72, 73
Verb Island Hypothesis 101

Watkins, T. A. 102–3
Watson, M. 150
Weissenborn, J. 101
Welsh Assembly government 52, 53, 58, 80, 143
Welsh language
  age of speakers x, 3, 4, 5, 55, 80–98, 118–45, 149, 152
  attitudes to x, 5, 43, 45, 53, 148, 149, 150, 151, 153, 155, 158–61, 163–4
  as community language x, xi, 4, 6, 55, 82, 90, 91–2, 93, 95–8, 149, 152–3, 163
  as first language 69, 73, 75, 92, 107, 110, 111–12
  grammar of 102–4, 105–12
  numbers of Welsh speakers 5, 80, 81, 82, 96, 118, 119, 127, 133, 137, 144
  percentages of Welsh speakers 5, 80, 81, 82–4, 85–95, 118–19,

122, 125, 126–8, 129–3, 144, 145, 149, 152, 154
as second-language 69, 73, 75, 92, 110–12, 151, 155, 156, 160
and social networks x, 4, 80–1, 82–98
and tourism 83, 84, 149, 150, 151–2, 164
and traditionally Welsh-speaking area x, 4, 5, 118–19, 122–3, 128–31, 132, 133–4, 136, 137, 142–3, 144, 148, 153, 163
and *passim*
Welsh Language Act (1993) 2–3, 6, 36–60, 80, 149
Welsh Language Board (WLB) 2, 6, 36–7, 38–9, 42, 45, 46, 47, 48–9, 51–2, 54, 56–7, 59–1, 80–1, 82, 151, 164
Welsh language schemes (WLS) 38–54, 56–7, 58–9
Welsh Language Measure (2010) 6, 54
Welsh-medium schools 3, 28, 61, 77–8, 81–2, 84, 86, 107, 111
Wenger, E. 22

Wenger, G. C. 150
Wenglish 64
Westminster government 38, 53, 57
Whitehaven 50
Wilcox, S. 123
Williams, Cen 74
Williams, Colin H. 2–3, 36–60, 77, 167
Williams, Glyn x–xi, 1–2, 6, 7–35, 129
Williams, I. W. 62
Williams, M. 148, 149
Winter, S. G. 16–17
Wittgenstein, Ludwig 14, 22

Young, E. 143
Ysbyty Bronglais (Aberystwyth) 129
Ysbyty Glangwili (Carmarthen) 129
Ysbyty Gwynedd (Bangor) 129
Ysgol Gymraeg Aberystwyth 3, 61, 78
Ysgol Uwchradd Tregaron 152
Ysgol Ystalyfera 84
Ystradgynlais 82, 84, 86, 87, 88, 89, 93, 94, 95, 98